Texas
GoMath!

Grade 1

Assessment Guide

- **Prerequisite Skills Inventory**
- **Beginning-of-Year, Middle-of-Year, and End-of-Year Benchmark Tests**
- **Module Tests in TEXAS Assessment Format**
- **Individual Record Forms**
- **Correlations to Texas Essential Knowledge and Skills for Mathematics**

Contents

Tests and Record Forms

Unit 4

Unit 5 (Module 19)

Unit 6 (Module 20)

Overview of *Texas GO Math!* Assessment

How Assessment Can Help Individualize Instruction

The *Assessment Guide* contains several types of assessment for use throughout the school year. The following pages will explain how these assessments can help teachers evaluate children's understanding of the Texas Essential Knowledge and Skills (TEKS). This *Assessment Guide* also contains Individual Record Forms (IRF) to help guide teachers' instructional choices to improve children's performance. The record forms may be used to monitor children's progress toward their mastery of the Texas Essential Knowledge and Skills for this grade.

Diagnostic Assessment

Prerequisite Skills Inventory in the *Assessment Guide* should be given at the beginning of the school year or when a new child arrives. This short answer test assesses children's understanding of prerequisite skills. Test results provide information about the review or intervention that children may need in order to be successful in learning the mathematics related to the TEKS for the grade level. The IRF for the Prerequisite Skills Inventory provides suggestions for intervention based on the child's performance.

Beginning-of-Year Test in the *Assessment Guide*, is multiple-choice format and should be given early in the year to determine which skills for the current grade children may already understand. This benchmark test will facilitate customization of instructional content to optimize the time spent teaching specific objectives. The IRF for the Beginning-of-Year Test provides suggestions for intervention based on the child's performance.

Show What You Know in the *Student Edition* is provided for each unit. It assesses prior knowledge from previous grades as well as content taught earlier in the current grade. Teachers can customize instructional content using the suggested intervention options. The assessment should be scheduled at the beginning of each unit to determine if children have the prerequisite skills for the unit.

Formative Assessment

Are You Ready? items appear in the *Assessment Guide*. These are quick checks to determine if children have the prerequisite skills they need for a particular lesson in the *Texas GO Math! Student Edition*. They may be reproduced for each child or shown to the class on a document camera. If several children have trouble with the Are You Ready? items, teachers may wish to review concepts before teaching the next lesson.

Middle-of-Year Test in the *Assessment Guide* assesses the same TEKS as the Beginning-of-Year Test, allowing children's progress to be tracked and providing opportunity for instructional adjustments, when required. The test contains multiple-choice items.

Summative Assessment

Module and Unit Assessments in the *Texas GO Math! Student Edition* indicate whether additional instruction or practice is necessary for children to master the concepts and skills taught in the module or unit. These tests include constructed-response and multiple-choice items.

Module and Unit Tests in the *Assessment Guide* evaluate children's mastery of concepts and skills taught in the module or unit. There is a test for each module. When only one module comprises a unit, the unit test assesses the content in just that module. When there are multiple modules in a unit, there are designated module tests and a comprehensive unit test. These tests contain multiple-choice items.

End-of-Year Test in the *Assessment Guide* assesses the same TEKS as the Beginning- and Middle-of-Year Tests. The test contains multiple-choice items. It is the final benchmark test for the grade level. When children's performance on the End-of-Year Test is compared to performance on Beginning- and Middle-of-Year Tests, teachers are able to document children's growth.

Using Correlations to TEKS

The final section of the *Assessment Guide* contains correlations to the TEKS. To identify which items in the *Assessment Guide* test a particular TEKS, locate that TEKS in the chart. The column to the right will list the test and specific items that assess the TEKS. Correlations to TEKS are also provided in the Individual Record Form for each test.

Assessment Technology

Online Assessment System offers flexibility to individualize assessment for each child. Teachers can assign entire tests from the *Assessment Guide* or build customized tests from a bank of items. For customized tests, specific TEKS can be selected to test.

Multiple-choice and fill-in-the-blank items are automatically scored by the Online Assessment System. This provides immediate feedback. Tests may also be printed and administered as paper-and-pencil tests.

The same intervention resources are available in the Online Assessment System as in the *Assessment Guide*. So, whether children take tests online or printed from the Online Assessment System, teachers have access to materials to help children succeed in *Texas GO Math!*

Data-Driven Decision Making

Texas GO Math! allows for quick and accurate data-driven decision making so teachers will have more instructional time to meet children's needs. There are several intervention and review resources available with *Texas GO Math!* Every lesson in the *Student Edition* has a corresponding lesson in the *Texas GO Math! Response to Intervention Tier 1 Lessons* online resource. There are also *Tier 2 Skills* and *Tier 3 Examples* available for children who need further instruction or practice. For online intervention lessons, children may complete lessons in *Soar to Success Math*. These resources provide the foundation for individual prescriptions for students who need extra support.

Using Individual Record Forms

The *Assessment Guide* includes Individual Record Forms (IRF) for all tests. On these forms, each test item is correlated to the TEKS it assesses. There are intervention resources correlated to each item as well. A common error explains why a child may have missed the item. These forms can be used to:

- Follow progress throughout the year.
- Identify strengths and weaknesses.
- Make assignments based on the intervention options provided.

1. Which shows eight ones?

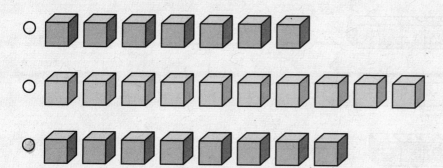

---

2. How many ones are in the number 9?

○ 9   ○ 10   ○ 5

- -

1. Which shows ten ones?

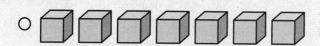

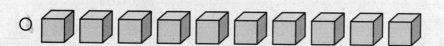

---

2. Which number has 10 ones?

○ 9   ○ 6   ◉ 10

1. Which shows another way to make ten ones?

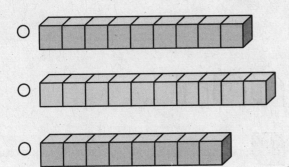

---

2. Which shows another way to write 10 ones?

○ 1 ten   ○ 8 ones   ○ 10 tens

- - - - - - - - - - - - - - - ✂ - - - - - - - - - - - - - - - - -

1. Which shows 1 ten 4 ones?

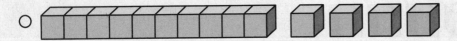

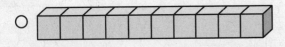

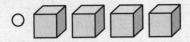

---

2. Which number has 1 ten 2 ones?

○ 8   ○ 2   ○ 12

1. Which shows 5 tens and 5 ones?

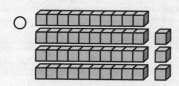

○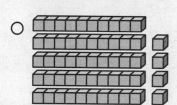

○

2. Which number has 6 tens 7 ones?

○ 76

○ 60

○ 67

✂ -

1. Which shows 13 two different ways?

○

○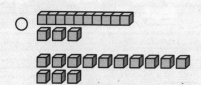

○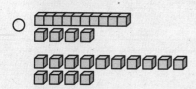

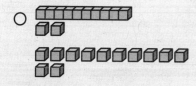

2. Which number is the same as 1 ten 5 ones?

○ 10

○ 16

○ 15

1. Which shows 2 tens?

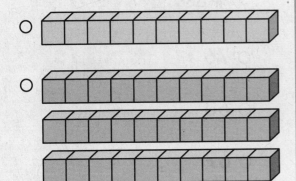

2. How many tens are in the number 40?

○ 4

○ 10

○ 5

1. Which number is greater than 23?

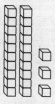

23

- ⊘ 32
- ○ 22
- ○ 14

2. Which number is greater than 34?

34

- ○ 30
- ○ 12
- ⊘ 44

1. Which number is less than 24?

24

- ○ 34
- ○ 16
- ⊘ 33

2. Which number is less than 31?

31

- ⊘ 22
- ○ 31
- ○ 32

1. Which symbol shows 21 is
equal to 21?

21   is equal to   21.

○ >

○ <

 =

2. Which symbol shows 42 is
greater than 22?

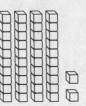

42   is greater than   22.

 >

○ <

○ =

✂ -

1. Which number is greater
than 81?

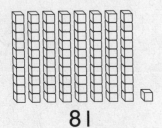

81

○ 80

○ 85

◎ 81

2. Which number is less
than 52?

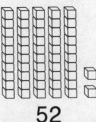

52

○ 25

○ 55

◎ 52

1. Which are shown in order from least to greatest?

   ⊘ 48, 69, 113

   ○ 69, 113, 48

   ○ 113, 69, 48

2. Which are shown in order from greatest to least?

   ○ 57, 95, 78

   ○ 57, 78, 95

   ⊘ 95, 78, 57

1. How many tens and ones make this number?

14
fourteen

- ○ 4 tens 1 one
- ◉ 1 ten 4 ones
- ○ 1 ten 14 ones

2. Which number is the same as 1 ten 2 ones?

- ◉ 12
- ○ 11
- ○ 21

✂ ─ ─ ─ ─ ─ ─ ─ ─ ─ ─ ─ ─ ─ ─

1. Which number does the model show?

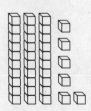

- ○ 63
- ◉ 36
- ○ 66

2. Which number is the same as 2 tens 8 ones?

- ◉ 28
- ○ 82
- ○ 27

Name _____

1. What is the sum?

$50 + 2 = \blacksquare$

○ 50

◉ 52

○ 2

2. How many tens and ones are in 85?

○ 5 tens 8 ones

◉ 8 tens 5 ones

○ 5 tens 5 ones

1. Which shows 1 and 3?

○ ▲ ▲ ▲ ▲ ▲

◉ ● ● ● ●

○ ■ ■ ■

2. How many circles are there?

○ 4

○ 5

◉ 6

✂ -

1. Which picture shows:
2 ducks and 3 more ducks

◉

○

○

2. Which is the sum?

○ 6

○ 5

◉ 7

1. Which picture shows:
Jill has 2 books. Then she
gets 1 more book.
How many books does Jill
have now?

○

○

○

2. Which addition sentence
matches the picture?

○ $3 + 1 = 4$

◉ $1 + 2 = 3$

○ $1 + 1 = 2$

---

1. Which shows the sum of
$5 + 3$?

○

◉

○

2. How many fish are there?

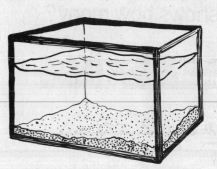

○ 1

○ 5

◉ 0

1. What is the sum?

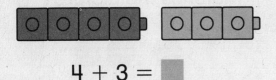

$$4 + 3 = \boxed{}$$

- ● 7
- ○ 9
- ○ 8

2. What is the sum?

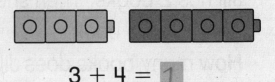

$$3 + 4 = \boxed{1}$$

- ○ 10
- ● 7
- ○ 9

1. Which addition sentence shows how many?

- ● $3 + 2 = 5$
- ○ $5 + 0 = 5$
- ○ $1 + 2 = 3$

2. Which addition sentence shows how many?

- ○ $4 + 2 = 6$
- ○ $5 + 0 = 5$
- ● $5 + 1 = 6$

1. Which addition sentence matches the model?

   ○ $10 = 7 + 3$

   ◉ $10 = 5 + 5$

   ○ $10 = 4 + 6$

___

2. Which is a way to make 10?

   ◉ $8 + 2$

   ○ $6 + 2$

   ○ $7 + 1$

1. How many cats are there?

- ○ 2
- ○ 4
- ◉ 3

2. How many cows are there?

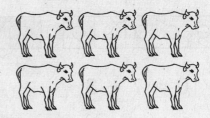

- ○ 4
- ◉ 6
- ○ 5

1. How many birds are left?

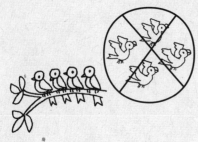

- ◉ 4
- ○ 8
- ○ 5

2. How many bees are left?

- ○ 6
- ○ 7
- ◉ 5

1. What is the difference?

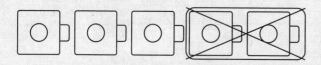

- ○ 4
- ◉ 3
- ○ 5

2. What is the difference?

$$9 - 3 = \blacksquare$$

- ◉ 6
- ○ 4
- ○ 5

✂ -

1. What is the difference?

$$7 - 5 = \blacksquare$$

- ○ 3
- ○ 1
- ◉ 2

2. Which subtraction sentence has a difference of 3?

- ○ $6 - 5 = \blacksquare$
- ◉ $5 - 3 = \blacksquare$
- ◉ $4 - 1 = \blacksquare$

1. Which subtraction sentence matches the picture?

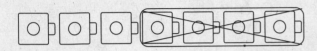

- ⊚ $7 - 4 = 3$

- ○ $8 - 4 = 4$

- ○ $7 - 2 = 5$

2. What is the difference?

$$8 - 7 = \blacksquare$$

- ○ 2

- ⊚ 1

- ○ 3

1. What is the difference?

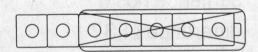

- ○ 3

- ○ 5

- ⊚ 2

2. Which subtraction sentence matches the picture?

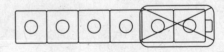

- ⊚ $6 - 2 = 4$

- ○ $6 - 1 = 5$

- ○ $6 - 0 = 6$

1. How many fish are there?

6 fish   and   3 more fish   fish

○ 6   ○ 3   ○ 9

2. What is the sum of 3 and 4?

○ 7   ○ 4   ○ 6

1. What is the sum for 3 + 0?

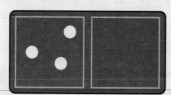

○ 3

○ 6

○ 0

2. There are 3 brown dogs and 3 black dogs. How many dogs are there?

○ 3

○ 6

○ 0

Name _____

1. Count on to solve $5 + 2$.
What is the sum?

- ○ 2
- ◉ 7
- ○ 5

2. Which is a doubles fact?

- ◉ $\begin{array}{r} 9 \\ +\ 9 \\ \hline 18 \end{array}$

- ○ $\begin{array}{r} 8 \\ +\ 1 \\ \hline 9 \end{array}$

- ○ $\begin{array}{r} 5 \\ +\ 0 \\ \hline 5 \end{array}$

Name _____

1. Which shows a way to
make 4?

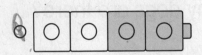

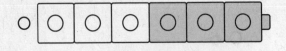

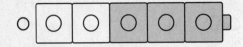

2. Which has the same sum
as $7 + 8$?

- ◉ $8 + 8 + 1$
- ○ $2 + 7 + 7$
- ○ $1 + 7 + 7$

1. Which fact is a doubles fact?

    ◉ 8 + 8 = 16

    ○ 9 + 2 = 11

    ○ 6 + 7 = 13

2. Which doubles fact helps you solve 5 + 6 = 11?

    ○ 4 + 4 = 8

    ◉ 5 + 5 = 10

    ○ 7 + 7 = 14

Name _Ailen_____

1. Solve.

8 bugs are flying. 2 more bugs fly with them. How many bugs are flying now?

    ○ 10

    ○ 8

    ○ 9

2. Which shows the same addends in a different order?

        3 + 7 = 10

    ○ 3 + 4 = 7

    ○ 6 + 3 = 9

    ○ 7 + 3 = 10

1. What number sentence does this model show?

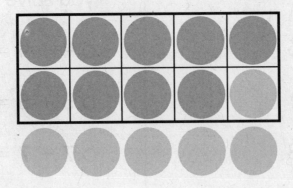

○ $10 + 5 = 15$

○ $10 - 1 = 9$

○ $10 + 1 = 11$

2. Which shows a way to make 10?

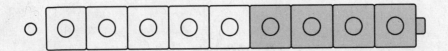

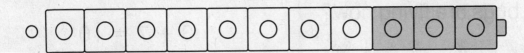

1. There are 8 turtles.
3 turtles walk away.
How many turtles are
there now?

  ○ 11

  ○ 3

  ○ 5

2. What is the difference?

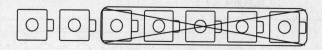

  ○ 2

  ○ 7

  ○ 1

1. Which number sentence
solves the problem?
There are 7 toy rockets.
4 rockets are red. The rest
are black. How many toy
rockets are black?

  ○ 7 − 4 = 3

  ○ 7 + 4 = 11

  ○ 7 − 2 = 5

2. How many fewer ☕ are
there?

  ○ 3 fewer ☕

  ○ 6 fewer ☕

  ○ 2 fewer ☕

1. Which shows a way to take apart 5?

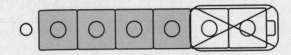
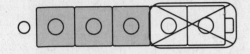
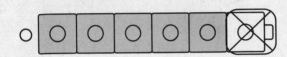

2. Which addition sentence helps you solve 9 − 3?

○ 3 + 6 = 9

○ 5 + 4 = 9

○ 2 + 1 = 3

1. Solve.
Abby has 8 stamps. Ben has 6 stamps. How many more stamps does Abby have than Ben?

○ 2

○ 3

○ 1

2. What is the difference for 6 − 0?

○ 1

○ 0

○ 6

1. Which shows a way to make a ten to subtract?

$$17 - 8 = \blacksquare$$

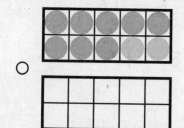

2. Which addition sentence helps you solve $5 - 3$?

    ○ $3 + 5 = 8$ ○ $3 + 2 = 5$ ○ $5 + 5 = 10$

1. Which number sentence solves the problem?
10 ducks are at the pond. All the ducks fly away. How many ducks are still at the pond?

    ○ $10 - 10 = 0$

    ○ $10 - 1 = 9$

    ○ $0 - 0 = 0$

2. Which subtraction sentence can you solve by using $9 + 7 = 16$?

    ○ $16 - 9 = \blacksquare$

    ○ $9 - 7 = \blacksquare$

    ○ $9 - 3 = \blacksquare$

Name _____

1. Which shows addition?

   ○ $20 - 10 = 10$

   ○ $15 - 9 = 6$

   ○ $5 + 7 = 12$

2. Which shows subtraction?

   ○ $14 - 6 = 8$

   ○ $10 + 6 = 16$

   ○ $9 + 8 = 17$

Name _____

1. Which addition fact shows 9 green apples plus 3 red apples?

   ○ $5 + 3 = 8$

   ○ $9 + 3 = 12$

   ○ $8 + 10 = 18$

2. Austin had 8 trucks. He got 7 more trucks. How many trucks does Austin have now?

   ○ 15

   ○ 9

   ○ 6

1. Which subtraction fact shows this story?
20 birds were on a branch. Ten birds flew away. How many birds were left?

○ $10 - 2 = 8$

○ $10 - 7 = 3$

○ $20 - 10 = 10$

2. Kristen had 17 stamps. She gave away 9 stamps. How many are left?

○ 17

○ 8

○ 9

1. Which shows the sum of $9 + 9$?

○ 8

○ 18

○ 3

2. Which shows the difference of $15 - 6$?

○ 15

○ 3

○ 9

1. What is the name of the coin?

○ nickel

○ dime

○ penny

2. Which coin is a nickel?

○

○

○

1. What is the total value?

○ 25¢

○ 30¢

○ 5¢

2. Which shows 30¢?

○

○

○

Name _____

1. What is the total value?

○ 4¢   ○ 21¢   ○ 26¢

2. Which shows 32¢?

○

○

○

✂

Name _____

1. Which shows 25¢?

○

○

○

2. What is the total value?

○ 40¢

○ 80¢

○ 70¢

1. Which shows the numbers in order counting forward?

   ○ 20, 21, 22, 23, 24, 25

   ○ 25, 20, 22, 24, 21, 23

   ○ 23, 25, 22, 21, 24, 20

2. What number begins this counting sequence?

   ▢, 32, 33, 34, 35, 36

   ○ 21

   ○ 31

   ○ 37

1. Which shows the numbers in order counting backward?

   ○ 20, 21, 22, 23, 24, 25

   ○ 25, 24, 23, 22, 21, 20

   ○ 21, 24, 22, 23, 25, 20

2. What number begins this counting sequence?

   ▢, 49, 48, 47, 46, 45

   ○ 40

   ○ 39

   ○ 50

Name _____

1. Which addition fact shows adding two?

○ 8 + 3 = 11

○ 10 + 2 = 12

○ 7 + 8 = 15

2. What number is two more than 11?

○ 13

○ 9

○ 12

- -

Name _____

1. Which addition fact shows adding five?

○ 6 + 6 = 12

○ 8 + 9 = 17

○ 7 + 5 = 12

2. What number is five more than 5?

○ 10

○ 9

○ 12

1. Which addition fact shows adding ten?

   ○ 6 + 8 = 14

   ○ 8 + 10 = 18

   ○ 7 + 9 = 16

2. What number is ten more than 15?

   ○ 10

   ○ 5

   ○ 25

1. What number is ten more than 10?

   ○ 20

   ○ 11

   ○ 30

2. What is the sum of 16 + 10?

   ○ 25

   ○ 26

   ○ 10

1. Which number is less than 29?

   ○ 48

   ○ 28

   ○ 30

2. Which number is greater than 44?

   ○ 43

   ○ 34

   ○ 45

Name _____

1. Which shows the addition sentence for the model?

○ $2 + 3 = 5$

○ $3 + 2 = 5$

○ $3 + 3 = 6$

2. What is the sum of $5 + 2$?

○ 7

○ 2

○ 5

Name _____

1. Which shows the subtraction sentence for the model?

○ $10 - 8 = 2$

○ $8 - 2 = 6$

○ $10 - 1 = 9$

2. What is the difference of $10 - 4$?

○ 4

○ 8

○ 6

1. How many more dogs are there than rabbits?

   ○ 4 more

   ○ 2 more

   ○ 3 more

2. How many fewer rabbits are there than dogs?

   ○ 2 fewer

   ○ 3 fewer

   ○ 1 fewer

There were some cupcakes. The chef baked 6 more cupcakes. Now there are 12 cupcakes.

1. How many cupcakes were there to begin with?

   ○ 6

   ○ 3

   ○ 5

2. Which number sentence matches the word problem?

   ○ $12 - 5 = 7$

   ○ $10 - 2 = 8$

   ○ $6 + 6 = 12$

1. Which shows the same addends as $3 + 2$ in a different order?

   ○ $2 + 5$

   ○ $2 + 3$

   ○ $5 + 1$

2. What is the sum of $3 + 2$?

   ○ 2

   ○ 5

   ○ 3

✂

1. Which two number pairs model the cubes?

   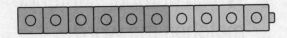

   ○ $8 + 1$ and $1 + 8$

   ○ $0 + 6$ and $6 + 0$

   ○ $6 + 4$ and $4 + 6$

2. What is the sum of $6 + 4$?

   ○ 6

   ○ 10

   ○ 4

1. Which shows two ways to make 10?

   ○ 8 + 1 and 5 + 4

   ○ 2 + 3 and 5 + 0

   ○ 6 + 4 and 5 + 5

2. What is the sum of
   1 + 1 + 1?

   ○ 3

   ○ 11

   ○ 8

---

1. Which addition sentence models the picture?

   ○ 6 + 2 = 8

   ○ 3 + 1 = 4

   ○ 4 + 3 = 7

2. Dee and Sam have 8 books. They get one more book. How many books do they have now?

   ○ 1

   ○ 9

   ○ 8

1. Which shows the addition
   fact for 3 and 2 more?

   ○ 2 + 1 = 3

   ○ 3 + 2 = 5

   ○ 3 + 1 = 4

2. Which shows the
   subtraction fact for
   4 take away 1 ?

   ○ 4 – 1 = 3

   ○ 5 – 3 = 2

   ○ 3 – 1 = 2

1. Which shows the matching
   subtraction problem for
   4 + 1 = 5?

   ○ 4 – 1 = 3

   ○ 5 – 2 = 3

   ○ 5 – 1 = 4

2. Which shows the matching
   addition problem for
   5 – 3 = 2?

   ○ 2 + 3 = 5

   ○ 3 + 1 = 4

   ○ 1 + 2 = 3

1. Which shows the matching subtraction problem for
$5 + 3 = 8$?

   ○ $5 - 3 = 2$

   ○ $8 - 3 = 5$

   ○ $9 - 1 = 8$

2. Which shows the matching addition problem for
$9 - 4 = 5$?

   ○ $4 + 1 = 5$

   ○ $2 + 4 = 6$

   ○ $5 + 4 = 9$

1. What number completes the addition sentence?

   $4 + \blacksquare = 5$

   ○ 1

   ○ 0

   ○ 2

2. What number completes the subtraction sentence?

   $5 - \blacksquare = 2$

   ○ 2

   ○ 1

   ○ 3

1. What number completes the number sentences?

$2 +$ $= 4$

$4 -$ ■ $= 2$

○ 3

○ 1

○ 2

2. What number completes the number sentences?

$3 -$ ■ $= 1$

$1 +$ ■ $= 3$

○ 2

○ 1

○ 3

1. Which expression shows 3 and 2?

○ $2 + 1$

○ $3 + 2$

○ $4 + 1$

2. What expression shows 5 take away 4?

○ $4 - 2$

○ $3 - 1$

○ $5 - 4$

Choose the best answer for each question.

1. Which shape is a triangle?

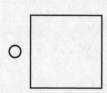 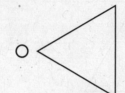 

2. Which shape has 4 sides?

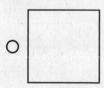  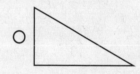

Choose the best answer for each question.

1. Which shape is curved?

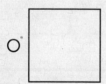 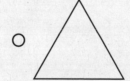 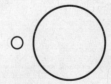

2. Which shape has 4 vertices?

○ triangle   ○ circle   ○ square

Choose the best answer for each question.

1. Which shape has 6 sides and 6 vertices?

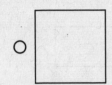 ○    ○   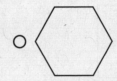 ○

---

2. How many vertices does a rhombus have?

○ 3   ○ 5   ○ 4

- -

Choose the best answer for each question.

1. How many △ do you use to make a ?

○ 3   ○ 5   ○ 4

---

2. How many △ do you use to make a ◇ ?

○ 4   ○ 2   ○ 3

Choose the best answer for each question.

1. Which shapes can combine to make
   this new shape?

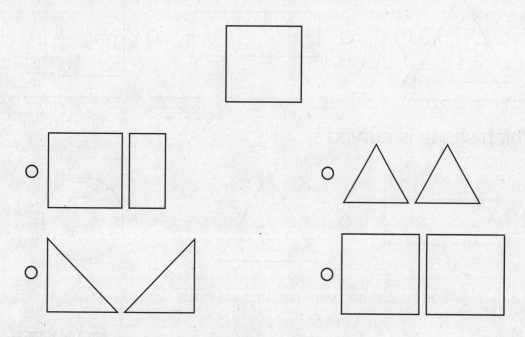

2. Which shapes can combine to make
   this new shape?

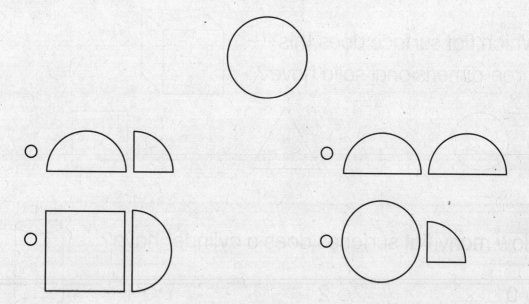

Choose the best answer for each question.

1. Which shape has 3 vertices and 3 sides?

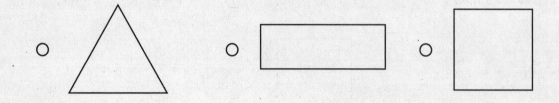

○   ○   ○

2. Which shape is curved?

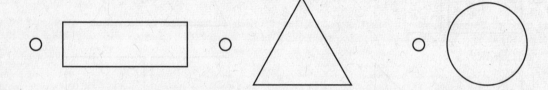

○   ○   ○

Choose the best answer for each question.

1. Which flat surface does this three-dimensional solid have?

 ○    ○   ○

2. How many flat surfaces does a cylinder have?

○ 0   ○ 2   ○ 1

Name _____

Choose the best answer for each question.

1. Which solid is a cone?

○ 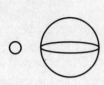   ○ 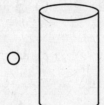   ○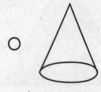

_____

2. How many flat surfaces does a sphere have?

○ 0   ○ 2   ○ 1

- -

Name _____

Choose the best answer for each question.

1. Which three-dimensional solid is a triangular prism?

○   ○   ○

_____

2. How many flat surfaces does a cube have?

○ 4   ○ 6   ○ 5

1. What is the name of this shape?

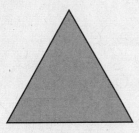

○ circle

○ rectangle

○ triangle

2. How many sides does a rectangle have?

○ 3

○ 4

○ 1

1. Which shape shows equal parts?

○

○

○

2. How many equal parts does this shape have?

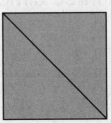

○ 4

○ 2

○ 0

1. Which shape shows two equal parts?

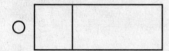

2. How many equal parts does this shape have?

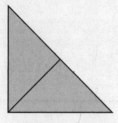

○ 2

○ 6

○ 4

1. Which crayon is longer than the line?

_____

2. Which crayon is shorter than the line?

_____

1. Which cube train is the same length as the pencil?

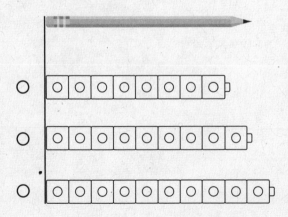

2. Which cube train is shorter than the pencil?

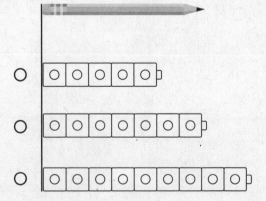

1. About how many 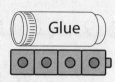 long is the glue stick?

Glue

○ about 2

○ about 4

○ about 3

2. About how many ▮ long is the book?

○ about 6 ▮

○ about 4 ▮

○ about 5 ▮

✂ -

1. Which measuring unit would you use fewest of to measure the same object?

○

○

○

2. Which measuring unit would you use most of to measure the same object?

○

○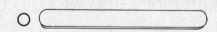

○

1. Which shows the numbers in order counting forward?

   o 3, 5, 6, 1, 2, 4

   o 1, 2, 3, 4, 5, 6

   o 5, 3, 4, 2, 6, 1

2. Which shows the numbers in order counting forward?

   o 1, 2, 9, 6, 8, 10, 7, 11

   o 11, 10, 12, 6, 8, 7, 9

   o 6, 7, 8, 9, 10, 11, 12

1. Which clock shows 5 o'clock?

o    o    o

2. Which clock shows 10 o'clock?

o    o    o

1. Which clock shows half past 1?

○    ○    ○

---

2. Which clock shows half past 8?

○    ○    ○

1. Which clock shows 4 o'clock?

○    ○    ○

---

2. Which clock shows half past 11?

○    ○    ○

Use the graph to answer the questions.

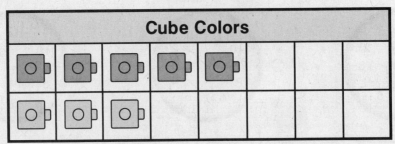

I. How many are there?

   ○ 6   ○ 3   ○ 5

2. How many are there?

   ○ 3   ○ 5   ○ 4

✂ -

Use the picture graph to answer the questions.

Our Favorite Fruit						
🍒 cherry	�star	☆	☆	☆		
🍐 pear	☆	☆	☆	☆	☆	☆

Each ☆ stands for I child.

I. How many children chose 🍐?

   ○ 6 children   ○ 10 children   ○ 4 children

2. How many fewer children chose 🍒 than 🍐?

   ○ 6 fewer   ○ 2 fewer   ○ 4 fewer

Use the picture graph to answer the questions.

Favorite Animal							
🐟 fish	○	○	○				
🐦 bird	○	○	○	○	○		
🐸 frog	○						

Each ○ stands for I child.

1. Which animal did the most children choose?

○ frog   ○ bird   ○ fish

2. How many children chose 🐦 and 🐟?

○ 5   ○ 8   ○ 6

Use the bar graph to answer the questions.

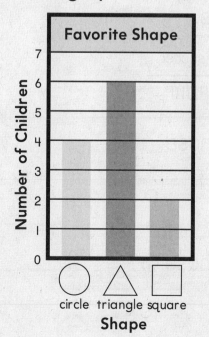

Favorite Shape

Number of Children

circle triangle square
Shape

1. How many more children chose △ than ☐?

○ 2   ○ 6   ○ 4

2. How many children chose ○?

○ 6   ○ 4   ○ 2

Use the bar graph to answer the questions.

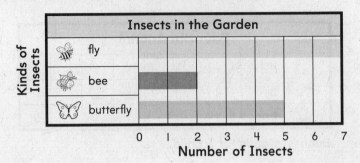

1. Which shows how many 🦋 are in the garden?

○ 2   ○ 7   ○ 5

_____

2. How many total insects are in the garden?

○ 7   ○ 14   ○ 12

- -

Name _____

Use the T-chart about children's favorite
outside activity to answer the questions.

🪁 kite flying	⚽ soccer
IIII III	IIII IIII

1. Which shows how many children chose 🪁?

○ 9   ○ 5   ○ 7

_____

2. Which shows how many children chose ⚽?

○ 7   ○ 9   ○ 5

Use the T-chart about the number of vegetables
the rabbit ate to answer the questions.

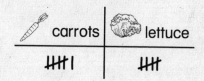

carrots	lettuce
⟊⟊⟊⟊|	⟊⟊⟊⟊

1. Which shows how many the rabbit ate?

   ○ 6

   ○ 11

   ○ 5

2. Which shows how many and 🥬 the
   rabbit ate?

   ○ 5

   ○ 11

   ○ 6

Name _____

1. What is the value of this coin?

○ 5¢   ○ 25¢   ○ 10¢

---

2. What is the value of these coins?

○ 30¢   ○ 3¢   ○ 15¢

- -

Name _____

1. Which shows the total cost of a pencil and a marker?

○ 6¢ + 6¢ = 12¢

○ 9¢ + 9¢ = 18¢

○ 6¢ + 9¢ = 15¢

---

2. What is the total cost of the kite and the ball?

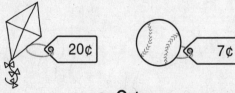

○ 27¢   ○ 9¢   ○ 90¢

1. Joe has 10¢ in his pocket and 5¢ in his hand. How much money does Joe have in all?

   ○ 50¢   ○ 15¢   ○ 20¢

2. Beth had 3 dimes and 1 nickel. She gave a dime to her sister. What is the value of the coins she has left?

   ○ 25¢   ○ 35¢   ○ 30¢

1. What is the total value of these coins?

   ○ 60¢   ○ 45¢   ○ 70¢

2. What is the total value of 1 quarter, 1 dime, and 1 nickel?

   ○ 40¢   ○ 45¢   ○ 35¢

Name _____

Write the correct answer.

1. Count forward. What is the missing number?

1, 2, 3, _____, 5

_____

2. Count backward. What is the missing number?

5, 4, 3, 2, _____

_____

3. What number is one more than 6?

6, _____

_____

4. What number is one less than 10?

10, _____

_____

5. Count the hats. Is 8 *less* than or *greater* than 7?

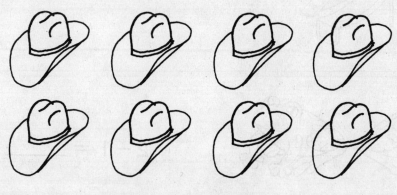

8 is _____ than 7.

GO ON ➡

Name _____

6. Count the fish. Is 12 *less* than or *greater* than 13?

12 is _____ than 13.

7. Al takes the 5-cube train apart. One train will have 2 cubes. How many cubes will the other train have?

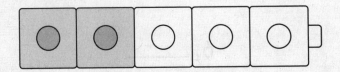

5 − 2 = _____

8.

2 + 1 = _____

9.

2 − 1 = _____

GO ON ➡

10. How many quarters are there?

_____

11. What is the missing number?

31	32	33	34	35	36	37	38	39	40
41	42	43	44	45	46		48	49	50

12. Count by tens. What is the missing number?

30, 40, 50, _____ , 70, 80

13. Which one is a square? Circle it.

GO ON →

14. Which object is shaped like a cube? Circle it.

box   can

---

15. What shape is the flat surface on a cylinder?

| circle | square | triangle |

_____

---

16. How many sides does a triangle have?

   _____ sides

---

17. What is the best name for this group of shapes?

| circles | squares | triangles |

Prerequisite Skills Inventory ⟶ GO ON

18. Which bracelet is longer? Circle it.

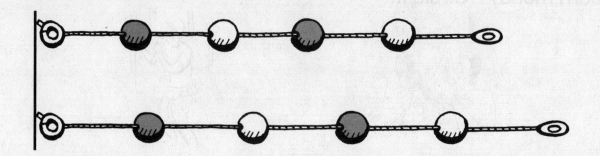

---

19. Which animal is shorter? Circle it.

---

20. Which object is lighter? Circle it.

---

21. Which pet did more people like?

Favorite Pet						
dog	○	○	○	○	○	○
cat	○	○	○	○		

GO ON ➡

Name _____

22. Which picture shows someone working to earn money? Circle it.

23. Which picture shows children working to earn money? Circle it.

24. Which picture shows a person who needs to know how to read addresses? Circle it.

25. Which food is a need? Circle it.

Fill in the bubble for the correct answer.

1. The model shows how many stickers David has. How many stickers does David have?

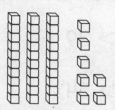

- ○ 3 tens 7 ones
- ○ 3 hundreds 7 tens
- ○ 7 tens 3 ones

2. Cal has 115 marbles. This model shows how many marbles Cal has.

Which shows this number?

- ○ 100 + 0 + 5
- ○ 10 + 5
- ○ 100 + 10 + 5

3. Amy counts 84 paper clips in the box. Which number is greater than 84?

- ○ 87
- ○ 82
- ○ 79

4. Ruby says a number greater than 52. The number has fewer tens than 70. Which could be this number?

- ○ 75
- ○ 61
- ○ 50

GO ON ➡

5. Which shows the numbers in order from least to greatest?

○ 97, 115, 65

○ 56, 40, 23

○ 18, 34, 102

6. Which shows how the numbers compare?

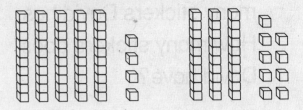

○ 54 > 39

○ 39 > 54

○ 39 = 39

7. Which number sentence does the model show?

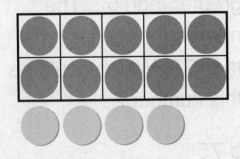

○ 10 + 10 = 20

○ 10 + 4 = 14

○ 10 + 3 = 13

8. 5 frogs and 2 more frogs

How many frogs are there?

○ 5

○ 7

○ 3

GO ON

9. The model shows one way to make 10.

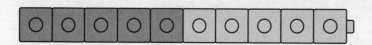

Which addition sentence matches the model?

○ $10 = 5 + 5$ ○ $10 = 0 + 10$ ○ $10 = 4 + 6$

---

10. Jerome has 8 peas on his plate. He eats 3 peas. How many peas are on his plate now?

○ 11

○ 7

○ 5

11. Eve has 5 red pens and 9 blue pens. Which number sentence shows how many pens Eve has?

○ $5 + 9 = 14$

○ $5 + 4 = 9$

○ $9 - 5 = 4$

---

12. Which problem matches the subtraction sentence $16 - 8 = 8$?

○ There are 16 red cars. There are 8 blue cars. How many cars are there?

○ There are 16 cars in the lot. 8 cars drive away. How many cars are there now?

○ There are 8 cars in the lot. 8 cars drive away. How many cars are there now?

13. What is the value of a dime?

○ 10¢   ○ 1¢   ○ 5¢

---

14. Harry has these pennies. He counts them by twos.

What is the total value of the coins?

○ 10¢   ○ 8¢   ○ 5¢

---

15. Count forward.

74, 75, 76, ▢, ▢, ▢

What numbers come next?

○ 78, 80, 82

○ 77, 78, 79

○ 75, 74, 73

16. Bella put the socks in pairs.

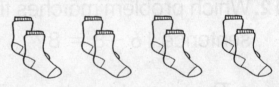

Which shows how to count the socks by twos?

○ 1, 2, 3, 4

○ 2, 4, 6, 8, 10

○ 2, 4, 6, 8

GO ON ➡

17. Emily has 72 crayons. She buys 10 more. Count forward by tens. How many crayons does Emily have?

○ 73

○ 82

○ 62

18. There are 5 sheep in the field. Then 6 more sheep join them. How many sheep are in the field?

○ 1

○ 10

○ 11

19. 6 cats and 3 more cats

$6 + 3 = $ ▩

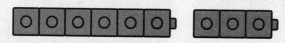

○ 3

○ 9

○ 2

20. Jaxon wrote the number sentence $7 + 3 = $ ▩. Which shows the same addends in a different order?

○ $3 + 7 = 10$

○ $7 - 3 = 4$

○ $4 + 6 = 10$

GO ON ➡

Name _____

21. Which subtraction fact is related to 7 + 6 = 13?

○ 13 − 8 = 5

○ 7 − 6 = 1

○ 13 − 6 = 7

22. Which shape has only 3 vertices?

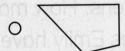
○

○

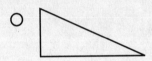
○

23. Mila has a shape. Which clue would help you guess the shape?

○ blue   ○ 6 vertices   ○ small

24. Circles are curved and closed shapes.

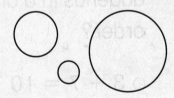

Which shape would be sorted into a group of circles?

○    ○    ○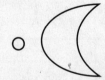

GO ON ➤

25. Ian has a marble. It is shaped like a sphere. How many flat surfaces does it have?

　　○ 0　　　　　○ I　　　　　○ 6

---

26. Which shapes can be combined to make this shape?

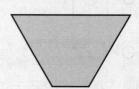

○ 　　　　○ 　　　　○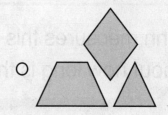

---

27. Aria is cutting a square sandwich into 2 equal parts. Which shows halves?

○

○

○

28. Which shape shows fourths?

○

○

○

29. Which object is longer than the string?

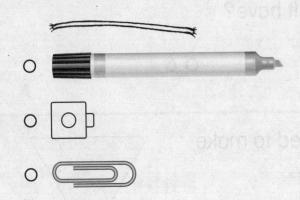

○

○

○

---

30. John measures this pencil with ■.
About how long is the pencil?

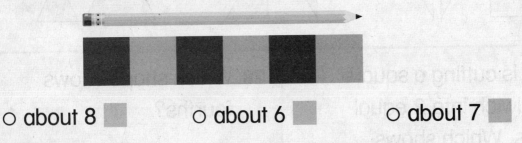

○ about 8 ■   ○ about 6 ■   ○ about 7 ■

---

31. Al measures from the desk to the door with .
Which unit will measure the same distance with fewer units?

○

○

○

32. Which ribbon is about 3 ■ long?

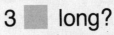

○

○

○

GO ON ➡

33. What time does the clock show?

- ○ 1 o'clock
- ○ 12 o'clock
- ○ 2 o'clock

34. Salem makes a T-chart. It shows each child's choice for favorite pet. Dogs win! Which could be her T-chart?

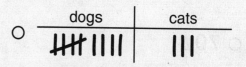

○

dogs	cats
IIII	HHT II

35. Kai drew ○ for each child's choice. 5 children chose red. 10 children chose blue. Which could be Kai's picture graph?

○

Our Favorite Color

red	○ ○ ○ ○ ○			
blue	○ ○			

○

Our Favorite Color

red	○ ○ ○ ○ ○	
blue	○ ○ ○ ○ ○ ○ ○ ○ ○ ○	

○

Our Favorite Color

red	○ ○ ○ ○ ○ ○ ○ ○ ○ ○
blue	○ ○ ○ ○ ○

36. Lou made this bar graph.

Which question could be answered by looking at the graph?

- ○ How many children wore a hat to school?
- ○ How many children have long hair?
- ○ Which hair color do the fewest children have?

GO ON ➡

37. Gabe earns 10¢ each time he feeds the dog. What does Gabe earn for feeding the dog 7 times?

○ 17¢

○ 70¢

○ 80¢

38. Remy is fixing the fence.

 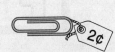

What is the total cost of the two things above that she will need?

○ 52¢

○ 5¢

○ 53¢

39. Ruth saves 5¢ each week for 5 weeks. How much money does Ruth save?

○ 10¢

○ 25¢

○ 20¢

40. Andy puts money in the sharing jar. He has 1 dime, 2 nickels, and 3 pennies. What is the total value of these coins?

○ 23¢

○ 18¢

○ 33¢

Fill in the bubble for the correct answer.

1. Juana is collecting pennies. She has 113 pennies. Which shows this number?

    ○ 1 ten 3 ones

    ○ 1 hundred 3 tens

    ○ 1 hundred 1 ten 3 ones

2. Karl has some cards. The model shows how many cards he has.

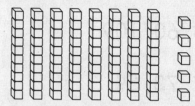

How many cards does Karl have?

    ○ 85

    ○ 58

    ○ 13

3. Shari writes the number 92. Which number is less than Shari's number?

    ○ 90

    ○ 97

    ○ 102

4. Use the number line to order the numbers. Which is the greatest number?

| 76 | 105 | 69 |

    ○ 76

    ○ 105

    ○ 69

GO ON ➡

5. Which shows the numbers in order from least to greatest?

○ 115, 89, 83

○ 58, 60, 109

○ 37, 73, 54

6. Which shows how the numbers compare?

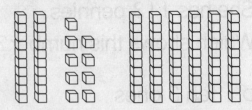

○ 29 < 60

○ 60 = 60

○ 60 < 29

7. Luis has 30 blocks. Nia has 8 blocks. How many blocks do they have?

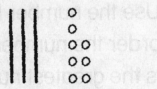

○ 11

○ 83

○ 38

8. 7 frogs. 2 frogs jump away.

How many frogs are there now?

○ 6

○ 5

○ 9

9. Which shows a way to make 10?

     ○ 6 + 3   ○ 4 + 7   ○ 2 + 8

---

10. Which shows a way to make a ten to subtract?

$$13 - 7 = \blacksquare$$

○ 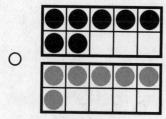   ○ 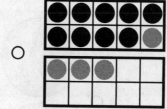   ○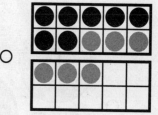

---

11. Lourdes has 8 markers. Carmen has 6 more markers than Lourdes. How many markers does Carmen have?

   ○ 2

   ○ 14

   ○ 12

12. Chung has 9 big rocks and 3 small rocks. Which addition fact shows how many rocks Chung has?

   ○ 9 + 3 = 12

   ○ 6 + 3 = 9

   ○ 3 + 3 = 6

GO ON ➡

13. Which coin has a value of 25¢?

○   ○   ○

14. LaToya has 1 dime. Which group of nickels
shows the same amount in a different way?

○   ○   ○

15. Count forward.

99, 100, 101, ▨, ▨, ▨

What numbers come next?

○ 102, 103, 104

○ 2, 3, 4

○ 112, 113, 114

16. Each hand has 5 fingers.

How many fingers are
on all of the hands? Skip
count by 5s.

○ 4   ○ 15   ○ 20

GO ON ➡

17. What number is 10 less than 107?

○ 97

○ 106

○ 108

18. There are 12 cats. 8 cats are white. The rest are black. How many cats are black?

$$12 - 8 = \blacksquare$$

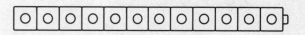

○ 9

○ 20

○ 4

19. What is the difference?

8 fish.   3 fish swim away.

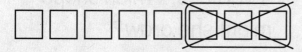

$$8 - 3 = \blacksquare$$

○ 5

○ 11

○ 6

20. What is the sum for $5 + 5 + 3$?

○ 15

○ 12

○ 13

GO ON ➡

21. Haya sees 2 white dogs.
She sees 4 brown dogs.
She sees 6 black dogs.
Which shows adding the
last two addends first?

○ 6 + 6

○ 2 + 10

○ 8 + 4

22. Royce is sorting shapes.
He makes a group of
shapes with 4 sides. Which
shape would **NOT** be
sorted into this group?

○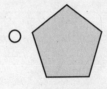

○

○

23. Rob has a shape. How
can he describe the shape
so you know it is a three-
dimensional solid?

○ 6 sides

○ 6 faces, 12 edges,
8 vertices

○ blue

24. Grace draws a shape
with 4 straight sides and
4 vertices. Which shape
might she draw?

○ triangle

○ rectangle

○ circle

GO ON

25. Which solid has both a flat and a curved surface?

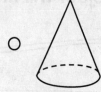

26. Leo makes this shape with blocks.

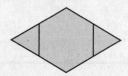

He will make a different shape with the same blocks. Which shape can he make?

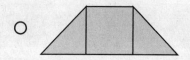

27. Jada cuts a square into 4 equal shares. Which is **NOT** a name for the equal shares?

○ fourths

○ quarters

○ halves

28. Which shape does **NOT** show halves?

○

○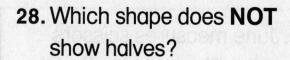

○

29. A box is the same length as this string.
Which object will fit in the box?

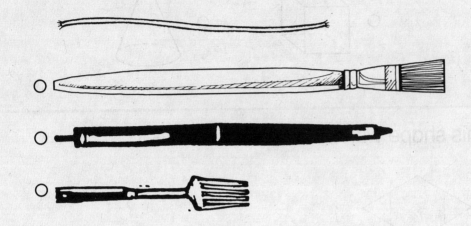

○

○

○

---

30. Eden measures this necklace with .
About how long is the necklace?

○ about 9   ○ about 8   ○ about 10

---

31. June measures scissors
with different units. Which
unit would she use the
fewest of?

○

○

○

32. About how many
long is the ribbon?

○ 3   ○ 5   ○ 4

GO ON ➡

Name _____

33. Look at the hour hand. What time is it?

○ half past 9

○ 9:00

○ 10:00

34. Look at the bar graph.

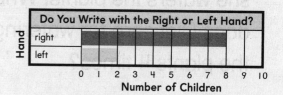

How many more children write with the right hand than the left hand?

○ 10   ○ 5   ○ 6

Use the data for 35–36.

Hopscotch or Tag?	
Ivy: hopscotch	Eli: hopscotch
Nora: tag	Ava: tag
August: tag	George: tag
Mae: tag	Jim: hopscotch

35. Which shows a T-chart for the data?

○
hopscotch	tag
III	IIII III

○
hopscotch	tag
IIII	III

○
hopscotch	tag
III	IIII

36. Which shows a bar graph for the data?

○
Each ☃ stands for 1 child.

○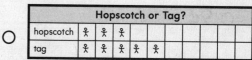

○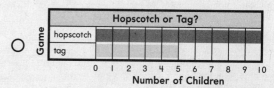

37. Didi earns 10¢ each time she waters the plants. What does Didi earn for watering the plants 4 times?

○ 40¢

○ 14¢

○ 50¢

38. Ira is making bracelets.

What is the total cost of the two things above that he will need?

○ 50¢

○ 37¢

○ 27¢

39. David has 15¢. He spends 6¢ to buy juice. How much money does David have left?

○ 9¢

○ 21¢

○ 8¢

40. Annie puts money in the sharing jar. She has 3 dimes and 5 pennies. What is the total value of these coins?

○ 8¢

○ 25¢

○ 35¢

Fill in the bubble for the correct answer.

1. Kyoko has 32 marbles.

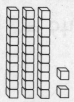

Which is a different way to show the same number?

○ 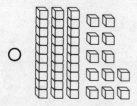　　○ 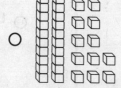　　○

2. Which is a different way to show the same number?

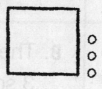

○ 113　　○ 130　　○ 103

3. Jude writes the number 87. Which number is less than Jude's number?

○ 84

○ 98

○ 90

4. What is the greatest number shown on the number line?

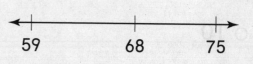
59　68　75

○ 59

○ 75

○ 68

GO ON

5. Use the number line to order the numbers.

| 113 | 87 | 93 |

←—————————————————→

Which shows the numbers in order from least to greatest?

○ 87, 93, 113

○ 113, 93, 87

○ 93, 87, 113

6. Which number is equal to 49?

49 = ▨

○ 59

○ 94

○ 49

7. 20 children are in the gym. 8 children are in the library. How many children are there?

○ 10

○ 82

○ 28

8. There are 5 acorns and 3 squirrels. How many more acorns are there?

○ 5 more

○ 2 more

○ 8 more

GO ON ▶

9. What is the sum for $4 + 2 + 6$?

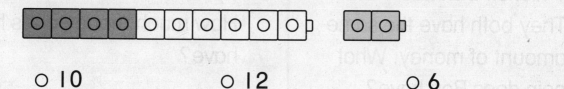

○ 10   ○ 12   ○ 6

---

10. Adam has 16 pretzels. He eats some pretzels. 8 pretzels are left. Which subtraction sentence shows how many pretzels Adam eats?

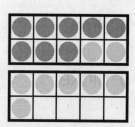

○ $16 - 8 = 8$ ○ $10 - 8 = 2$ ○ $8 - 8 = 0$

---

11. There are 18 apples. 9 apples are big. The rest are small. Which number sentence shows how many apples are small?

○ $9 - 9 = 0$

○ $18 - 8 = 10$

○ $18 - 9 = 9$

12. Which subtraction sentence matches the model?

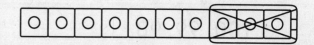

○ $10 - 7 = 3$

○ $10 - 3 = 7$

○ $7 - 3 = 4$

13. Vanita has 2 dimes and 1 nickel. Ben has 1 coin. They both have the same amount of money. What coin does Ben have?

○ 1 quarter

○ 1 dime

○ 1 nickel

14. Lamont counted 5 dimes by tens to find the value. How much money does he have?

○ 5¢

○ 50¢

○ 25¢

15. Count backward.

103, 102, 101, ▩, ▩, ▩

What numbers come next?

○ 102, 103, 104

○ 100, 90, 80

○ 100, 99, 98

16. There are 10 pennies in each bag.

How many pennies are there? Skip count by 10s.

○ 30

○ 3

○ 15

GO ON ➡

17. Look at the chart. What are the unknown numbers?

10 Less		10 More
■	85	■

○ 75 and 95 ○ 84 and 86 ○ 95 and 105

---

18. Len has 9 shells. Lydia has 6 shells. Which number sentence shows how many fewer shells Lydia has than Len?

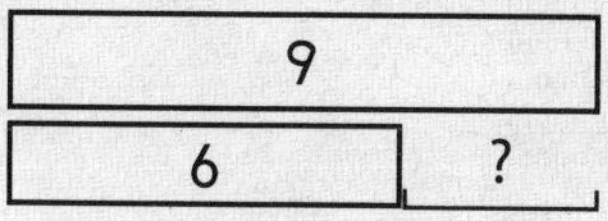

○ $9 - 6 = 3$ ○ $6 - 4 = 2$ ○ $9 + 6 = 15$

---

19. What number would make expressions of equal value?

$12 - 7 = 1 + ■$

○ 11

○ 5

○ 4

20. What number completes the related facts?

$7 + 7 = ■$ and $■ - 7 = 7$

○ 7

○ 15

○ 14

GO ON

21. Which addition fact helps you solve $13 - 8$?

○ $6 + 2 = 8$

○ $5 + 8 = 13$

○ $3 + 8 = 11$

22. Fiona is sorting shapes. She makes this group.

Which shape would **NOT** be sorted into this group?

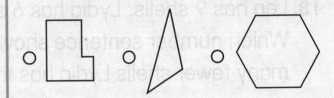

23. Rose has a shape. Which clue would **NOT** help you guess the shape?

○ 2 flat surfaces

○ big

○ curved surface

24. Nolan draws a shape with 4 straight sides that are all the same length. Which shape might he draw?

○ square

○ triangle

○ circle

GO ON

25. Bud has a toy that is shaped like a cylinder. How many flat surfaces does the toy have?

○ 0

○ 1

○ 2

26. Which two shapes can make a square?

○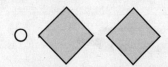

○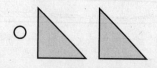

○

27. Alexa cuts a circle into 4 equal shares. Which is **NOT** a name for the shares?

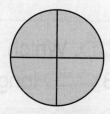

○ halves

○ fourths

○ quarters

28. Which rectangle shows 4 unequal parts?

○

○

○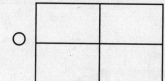

GO ON

29. A box is the same length as this string.
Which object will fit in the box?

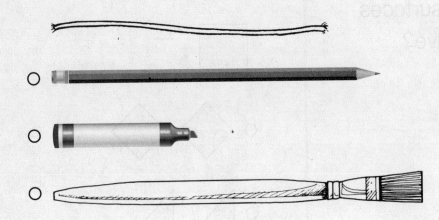

○

○

○

---

30. Mari measures this bracelet with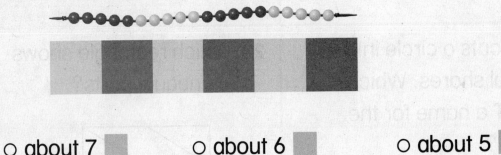
About how long is the bracelet?

○ about 7 ▢   ○ about 6 ▢   ○ about 5 ▢

---

31. Robin measures a spoon.
Which unit would he use
the greatest number of?

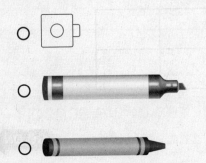

○

○

○

32. Use  Which ribbon is
about 3 🖇 long?

○

○

○

GO ON ▶

33. What time does the clock show?

○ half past 12

○ 2 o'clock

○ half past 2

34. How many more children chose blue than pink?

pink	blue
II	ℍ IIII

○ 7

○ II

○ 9

35. Tory has 10 toy trucks. 3 trucks are blue. 7 trucks are green. Which could be Tory's graph?

○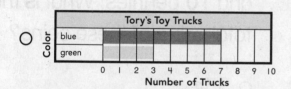

○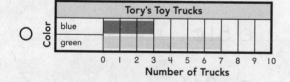

○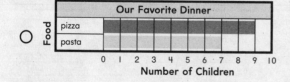

36. Ada made this bar graph.

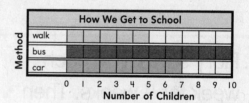

Which question could be answered by looking at the graph?

○ How many children like pizza for lunch?

○ How many children have long hair?

○ How do the most children get to school?

GO ON ➡

37. Shima earns 5¢ for each window she washes. What does Shima earn for washing 4 windows?

○ 20¢

○ 9¢

○ 25¢

38. Lilly is painting a house.

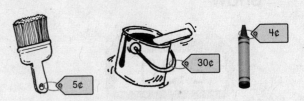

What is the total cost of the two things above that she will need?

○ 34¢

○ 35¢

○ 9¢

39. Rory saves 10¢ each week for 4 weeks. Then he spends 20¢ to buy a magazine. How much money does Rory have left?

○ 6¢

○ 60¢

○ 20¢

40. Jaleel puts money in the sharing jar. He has 5 dimes and 10 pennies. What is the total value of these coins?

○ 35¢

○ 51¢

○ 60¢

STOP

Fill in the bubble for the correct answer.

1. Which shows the same
number?

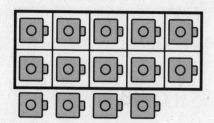

- ○ I ten 14 ones
- ○ I ten 4 ones
- ○ I one 4 tens

2. John counts 19 children in
class. Which shows how
many children are in class?

- ○ I ten 6 ones
- ○ I ten 3 ones
- ○ I ten 9 ones

3. Sarah got the ball in the basket 10 times.
Which model shows 10?

○ 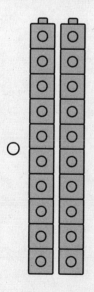   ○ 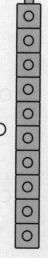   ○

GO ON ➡

4. The model shows how many toy cars Don has. How many toy cars does Don have?

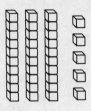

○ 35   ○ 53   ○ 38

5. Which picture shows 1 hundred 1 ten 7 ones?

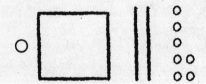

○

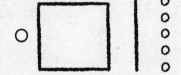

○

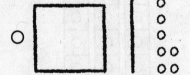

○

6. Juan has 27 paintbrushes.

Which is a different way to show the same number?

○

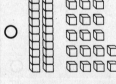

○

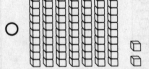

○

7. Rachel has 58 crayons in a box. How many tens and ones are in 58?

○ 8 tens 5 ones

○ 5 tens 8 ones

○ 80 tens 5 ones

---

8. Eva counts rocks during her walk. There are 60 + 3 rocks. Which model shows her number?

---

9. Julie counts apples in the yard. There are 1 hundred 1 ten 8 ones. How many apples did she count?

○ 102

○ 118

○ 108

GO ON →

10. Ben has a box of shells. The model shows how many shells are in the box. How many shells does Ben have?

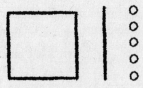

○ 100

○ 105

○ 115

11. The model shows how many minutes it takes Josie to get to school.

What number does the model show?

○ 15

○ 6

○ 30

12. Which is a different way to show the same number?

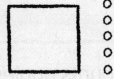

○ 150

○ 105

○ 155

STOP

Fill in the bubble for the correct answer.

1. Amy counts 37 flowers in the garden.
   Which number is greater than 37?

   ○ 42   ○ 35   ○ 33

2. There are fewer than 45 chairs in the room.
   Which number is less than 45?

   ○ 47   ○ 54   ○ 42

3. Sally says a number greater than 26.
   The number has fewer tens than this model.

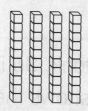

   Which number did Sally say?

   ○ 22   ○ 36   ○ 45

GO ON

4. Bonnie sees some rabbits. The number of rabbits is less than 37. How many rabbits does Bonnie see?

      ○ 39   ○ 38   ○ 35

---

5. John has 92 cards. Paul has 112 cards. Wendy has 107 cards. Which shows the numbers of cards in order from greatest to least?

    ○ 112, 107, 92

    ○ 92, 107, 112

    ○ 107, 92, 112

---

6. There are 12 fish in one tank, 36 in another, and 8 in another. Which shows the numbers of fish in order from least to greatest?

    ○ 12, 36, 8

    ○ 8, 12, 36

    ○ 36, 23, 8

7. Which shows the numbers in order
from least to greatest?

○ 48, 50, 20

○ 20, 48, 50

○ 50, 48, 20

8. What is the greatest number shown on this
number line?

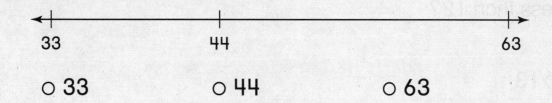

○ 33   ○ 44   ○ 63

9. Which shows the numbers in order
from greatest to least?

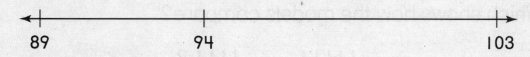

○ 103, 94, 89

○ 103, 89, 94

○ 89, 94, 103

GO ON

10. Which shows how the models compare?

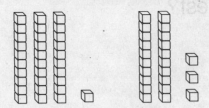

○ 31 < 23

○ 31 > 23

○ 33 = 23

---

11. Dan catches 12 fish today. Which number is less than 12?

○ 13

○ 21

○ 10

---

12. Which shows how the models compare?

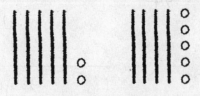

○ 52 > 45   ○ 45 = 45   ○ 52 < 45

Fill in the bubble for the correct answer.

1. What is the sum?

$$\begin{array}{r} 10 \\ +\ 3 \\ \hline \end{array}$$

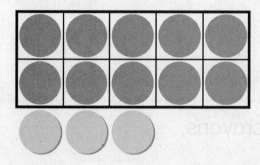

- ○ 31
- ○ 13
- ○ 3

2. What number sentence does the model show?

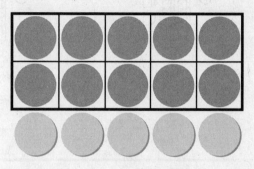

- ○ $10 + 5 = 15$
- ○ $10 + 1 = 11$
- ○ $10 + 4 = 14$

3. Cho has 40 baseball cards. She has 3 football cards. Which number sentence shows how many cards there are in all?

- ○ $30 + 4 = 34$
- ○ $4 + 3 = 7$
- ○ $40 + 3 = 43$

GO ON ➡

4. Which shows $20 + 6 = 26$?

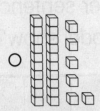   ○   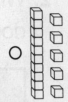   ○   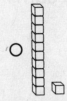   ○

5. Lou has 30 crayons. Fran has 7 crayons.

How many crayons do they have in all?

○ 73   ○ 10   ○ 37

6. Tess has 20 red apples and 1 green apple.
Which picture shows how many apples she has?

○   ○   ○

GO ON ➡

7. What is the sum?

$$\begin{array}{r} 10 \\ + \ 9 \\ \hline \end{array}$$

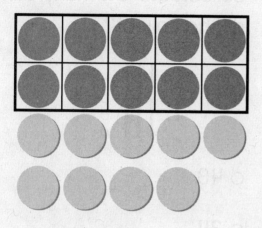

○ 15

○ 13

○ 19

8. There are 2 roses and 10 tulips in a vase. Which shows 10 + 2?

○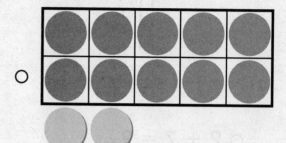

○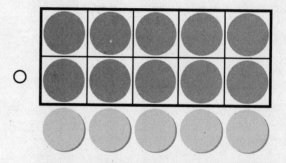

○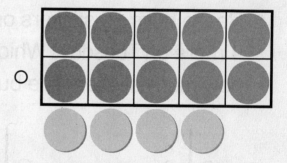

9. How could Paul draw tens and ones to show 10 + 7 = 17?

○    ○   ○

10. Which number sentence does this picture show?

○ 70 + 2 = 72

○ 2 + 7 = 9

○ 20 + 7 = 27

11. Alexi collected cans for school. He drew a picture to show how many he collected. How many cans did he collect?

○ 43

○ 34

○ 70

12. Reese buys 10 stickers on Monday. She buys 4 more on Tuesday. Which picture shows how many stickers she buys?

STOP

Fill in the bubble for the correct answer.

1. There are 5 children at the zoo.
Then 2 more children join them.

Which number sentence shows how many
children are at the zoo?

○ $5 + 2 = 7$

○ $5 + 3 = 8$

○ $5 + 4 = 9$

---

2. Pete puts 3 plates on the
table. Then he puts 3 more
plates on the table. Which
model shows how many
plates are on the table?

○

○

○

3. There are 3 cows in the
field. Then 2 more cows
join them.

How many cows are there
in the field?

○ 2   ○ 5   ○ 3

GO ON

4. There are 4 red umbrellas. There are
2 blue umbrellas. How many umbrellas
are there?

    ○ 6   ○ 4   ○ 2

---

5. The model shows one way to make 10.

Which addition sentence matches the model?

   ○ 10 = 10 + 0

   ○ 10 = 6 + 4

   ○ 10 = 5 + 5

---

6. Which shows a way to make 10?

   ○ 5 + 4

   ○ 9 + 0

   ○ 7 + 3

7. Gil knows that $3 + 4 = 7$. Which shows the same addends in a different order?

○ $6 + 1 = 7$

○ $4 + 3 = 7$

○ $5 + 2 = 7$

---

8. There are 4 red cars and 2 blue cars. Which model shows how many cars there are?

○

○

○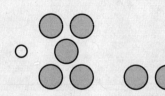

9. Jill has 5 balloons. Bob has 3 balloons. How many balloons are there?

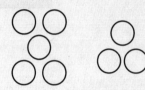

○ 7

○ 6

○ 8

GO ON

10. Mrs. Brown has 3 small books and 6 large books. Which number sentence shows how many books she has?

    ○ $3 + 6 = 9$

    ○ $6 - 3 = 3$

    ○ $6 + 6 = 12$

11. 2 bluebirds and 6 more bluebirds

    $2 + 6 = $ ▨

    ○ 5

    ○ 8

    ○ 4

12. Jenna has 10 oranges. Jose has none. Which number sentence shows how many oranges they have altogether?

    ○ $0 + 0 = 0$

    ○ $10 + 1 = 11$

    ○ $10 + 0 = 10$

Name _____

Fill in the bubble for the correct answer.

1. Karla sees 4 birds on a fence. 4 birds fly away.

Which number sentence shows how many birds are left?

○ $4 + 4 = 8$

○ $4 - 4 = 0$

○ $4 - 0 = 4$

2. There are 8 bugs on a stick. 4 bugs walk away. Then 1 more bug walks onto the stick. How many bugs are there now?

○ 5

○ 13

○ 4

---

3. Jaden has 5 mugs and 3 plates.

How many more mugs does Jaden have?

○ 3 more mugs

○ 5 more mugs

○ 2 more mugs

4.

How many fewer  are there?

○ 7 fewer

○ 4 fewer

○ 3 fewer

---

5. There are 9 cars.
Then 2 cars drive away.
How many cars are there now?

○ 6

○ 7

○ 11

6. There are 6 carrots.
Tim eats 5.
How many carrots are there now?

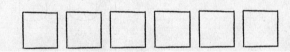

○ 1

○ 6

○ 5

7. How many fewer 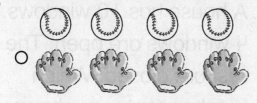 are there?

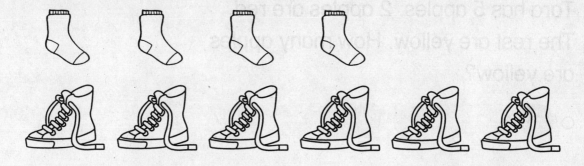

○ 2 fewer   ○ 4 fewer   ○ 10 fewer

---

8. There are 8 balls and 4 mitts. Which picture shows how many more balls there are?

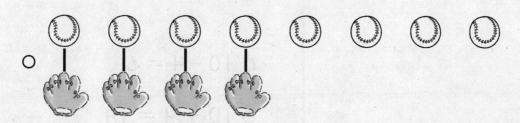

---

9. Which shows a way to take apart 8?

○ 10 − 2 = 8   ○ 8 + 3 = 11   ○ 8 − 3 = 5

GO ON ➡

10. Which model shows how to solve this problem?

Tara has 5 apples. 2 apples are red.
The rest are yellow. How many apples
are yellow?

11. Ralph has 9 pencils. 3 are long. The rest are short. How many pencils are short?

- ○ 12
- ○ 6
- ○ 3

12. A house has 10 windows. 4 windows are open. The rest are closed. Which number sentence shows how many windows are closed?

- ○ 10 − 4 = 6
- ○ 10 + 4 = 14
- ○ 3 + 7 = 10

Fill in the bubble for the correct answer.

1. Huang has 43 marbles.

   Which is a different way to show 43?

   ○ 4 tens 3 ones   ○ 3 tens 4 ones   ○ 43 tens

---

2. Isla has 115 marbles. Which one
   does **NOT** show this number?

   ○ $100 + 10 + 5$

   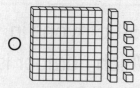

   ○ $15 + 10$

---

3. Which way does **NOT** show the same number?

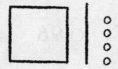

   ○ 1 hundred 1 ten 4 ones

   ○ 104

   ○ $100 + 10 + 4$

GO ON

4. Which model shows the number?

107

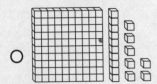

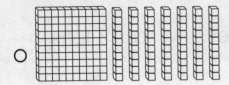

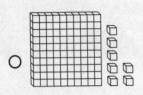

---

5. What number does the picture show?

○ 102

○ 120

○ 112

6. There are 64 crayons in the box. Which number is greater than 64?

○ 12

○ 24

○ 96

GO ON ➡

7. Shari writes the number 75.
Which number is less than 75?

   ○ 67

   ○ 78

   ○ 81

---

8. Which shows the numbers in order
from least to greatest?

   ○ 79, 90, 116

   ○ 34, 56, 29

   ○ 87, 65, 43

---

9. Which number could belong at the dot?

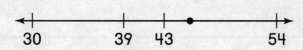

   30   39 43   54

   ○ 40

   ○ 53

   ○ 45

GO ON

10. Which number sentence does the model show?

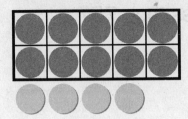

- ○ $10 - 4 = 6$
- ○ $10 + 4 = 14$
- ○ $4 + 6 = 10$

11. There are 7 boats. 4 sail away. How many boats are there now?

- ○ 11
- ○ 3
- ○ 6

12. There are 6 bees and 8 flowers.

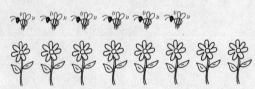

How many more flowers are there?

- ○ 2 more flowers
- ○ 3 more flowers
- ○ 4 more flowers

13. Ramesh has 5 pennies. Then he finds 4 more. How many pennies does Ramesh have now?

○ 9   ○ I   ○ 10

14. How many kittens are there?

6 kittens   and   I more kitten   ▮ kittens

○ 5

○ 7

○ 8

15. How many are there now?

8 butterflies   2 butterflies fly away.   ▮ butterflies now

○ 10   ○ 8   ○ 6

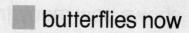

16. How many fewer are there?

○ 1 fewer   ○ 4 fewer   ○ 2 fewer

---

17. There are 5 red apples and
5 green apples. Which picture
shows how many apples there are?

○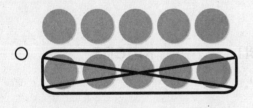

○

○

---

18. Jess sees 9 trucks. 1 truck is small.
The rest are big. Which number sentence
shows how many trucks are big?

○ $10 - 1 = 9$ ○ $9 - 1 = 8$ ○ $9 + 1 = 10$

Fill in the bubble for the correct answer.

1. Count on. What is the sum?

$$\blacksquare = 9 + 2$$

○ 7

○ 10

○ 11

---

2. Zoe has 6 pink bows. She has 6 blue bows. How many bows are there?

○ 12

○ 11

○ 10

---

3. Which has the same sum as $5 + 6$?

○ $5 + 5 + 2$

○ $6 + 6 + 1$

○ $5 + 5 + 1$

GO ON ➡

Name _____

4. Ryan wants to find $5 + 8$. He makes a ten to add. Which addition fact does he use?

○ $2 + 3 + 7 = 12$

○ $10 + 3 = 13$

○ $5 + 10 = 15$

5. Which number sentence matches the model?

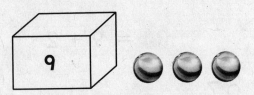

○ $9 + 3 = 12$

○ $8 + 4 = 12$

○ $9 - 3 = 6$

6. A squirrel finds 8 big acorns. It finds 8 small acorns. Which doubles fact shows how many acorns there are?

○
$$\begin{array}{r} 10 \\ + 6 \\ \hline 16 \end{array}$$

○
$$\begin{array}{r} 8 \\ + 8 \\ \hline 16 \end{array}$$

○
$$\begin{array}{r} 9 \\ + 9 \\ \hline 18 \end{array}$$

GO ON ➡

7. There are 8 red crayons. There are 8 blue crayons. There is I yellow crayon. How many crayons are there?

○ 17

○ 19

○ 16

8. Which doubles fact can **NOT** help to solve 7 + 6?

○ 7 + 7 = 14

○ 6 + 6 = 12

○ 8 + 8 = 16

9. Which number sentence does this model show?

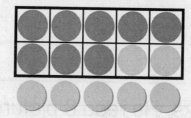

○ 10 − 2 = 8

○ 10 + 5 = 15

○ 8 + 5 = 13

10. Which shows how to make a ten to solve $9 + 4$?

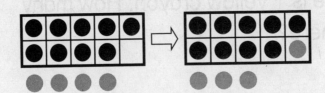

○ $9 + 4 + 3$ ○ $9 + 1 + 3$ ○ $10 - 1$

---

11. Elena has 9 bells and 5 whistles. Which model shows how she can make a ten to solve $9 + 5$?

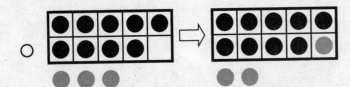

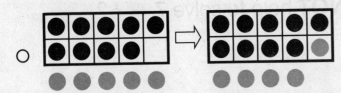

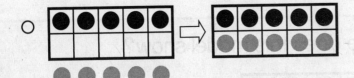

---

12. Jack read 4 story books. He read 8 picture books. How many books did Jack read?

○ 14   ○ 4   ○ 12

Fill in the bubble for the correct answer.

1. Count back. What is the difference?

$$\blacksquare = 10 - 3$$

○ 7

○ 13

○ 8

2. Tal wants to solve $9 - 6$. Which addition fact will help him subtract?

○ $6 + 3 = 9$

○ $3 + 3 = 6$

○ $9 + 6 = 15$

3. Which subtraction sentence can you solve by using $5 + 7 = 12$?

○ $10 - 7 = \blacksquare$

○ $7 - 5 = \blacksquare$

○ $12 - 5 = \blacksquare$

GO ON

4. What is $8 - 5$?

- ○ 13
- ○ 3
- ○ 5

5. Alita is finding $17 - 8$. Which addition fact will help her subtract?

- ○ $7 + 8 = 15$
- ○ $4 + 4 = 8$
- ○ $8 + 9 = 17$

6. Jake has 7 apples in a basket. He throws away 1 apple. Then he eats 2 apples. How many apples are in the basket now?

- ○ 6
- ○ 4
- ○ 10

GO ON

7. Which shows a way to make a ten to subtract?

$$15 - 8 = \blacksquare$$

○ 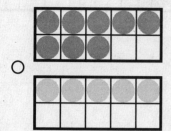   ○ 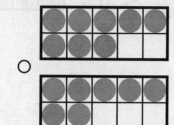   ○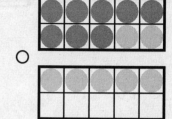

---

8. Liam had 14 toy dinosaurs. He gave 6 toy dinosaurs to Ethan. How many toy dinosaurs does Liam have now?

○ 8

○ 10

○ 14

---

9. Ava had 13 stuffed animals. She gave away some of them. Now she has 9 stuffed animals. How many did Ava give away?

○ 5

○ 4

○ 6

GO ON →

10. Which way shows making a ten to solve $16 - 7$?

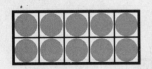 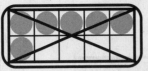 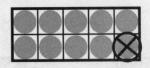 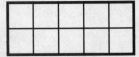

    ○ $16 - 6 - 1$

    ○ $10 - 1$

    ○ $16 - 6$

---

11. Kyoko has 17 toy cars. Which subtraction sentence shows how to subtract 9 by making a ten?

    ○ $17 - 10 = 7$

    ○ $17 - 7 - 2 = 8$

    ○ $17 - 9 = 8$

---

12. Which subtraction sentence is shown by the model?

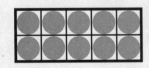 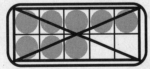 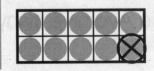 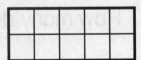

    ○ $8 - 1 = 7$

    ○ $10 - 1 = 9$

    ○ $18 - 9 = 9$

Name _____

Fill in the bubble for the correct answer.

1. Lara fills 7 cups with juice. Then she fills 8 more cups. How many cups does Lara fill?

Which tells how to solve the problem?

○ Subtract. ○ Add. ○ Count on.

2. Cal has 5 pears. He picks 4 more pears. Then Lucy gives him 6 more pears.

Which shows how to find the number of pears with counters?

3. Which picture matches 2 + 7?

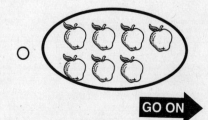

4. Sergio makes 6 berry pancakes and 5 nut pancakes.

Which number sentence shows how many pancakes Sergio makes?

○ $6 - 5 = 1$

○ $6 + 6 = 12$

○ $6 + 5 = 11$

5. Ali sees 3 chipmunks. Jim sees 9 more chipmunks than Ali.

Which number sentence shows how many chipmunks they see?

○ $3 + 9 = 12$

○ $9 - 3 = 6$

○ $3 + 9 + 3 = 15$

6. Owen has 18 baseball cards. He gives 9 of the cards to Dara. How many cards does Owen have now?

Which tells how to solve the problem?

○ Subtract 9 from 18.

○ Add 18 and 9.

○ Subtract 8 from 9.

GO ON

Assessment Guide
© Houghton Mifflin Harcourt Publishing Company

7. Adam blows up 3 red balloons. He blows
up 5 green balloons. Then 6 balloons pop.
How many balloons does Adam have now?

Which tells how to solve the problem?

○ Add 3 and 6. Subtract 5.

○ Add 3, 5, and 6.

○ Add 3 and 5. Subtract 6.

8. Wen found 9 big shells and 3 small shells.
She gave 9 shells to Darius. How many
shells does Wen have now?

○ 12   ○ 3   ○ 13

9. Which drawing matches the fact 10 − 8?

○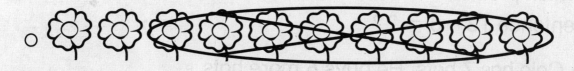

○

○

GO ON ➡

10. Lauren paints 15 pictures. She
    gives away 8 pictures to friends.

    Which number sentence shows
    how many pictures Lauren has now?

    ○ $8 + 5 = 13$ ○ $15 - 8 = 7$ ○ $15 - 5 = 10$

---

11. Which problem matches the
    addition sentence $9 + 8 = 17$?

    ○ Tiara has 9 rag dolls. She has 8 baby
       dolls. How many dolls does she have?

    ○ Tiara has 9 rag dolls. She gives away
       8 dolls. How many dolls does she have now?

    ○ Tiara has 9 dolls. Amy has 8 fewer dolls
       than Tiara. How many dolls do they have?

---

12. Which problem matches the subtraction
    sentence $13 - 6 = 7$?

    ○ Cole has 7 hats. He buys 6 more hats.
       How many hats does he have now?

    ○ Cole has 13 hats. Dan has 6 hats.
       How many hats do they have?

    ○ Cole has 13 hats. He gives away 6 hats.
       How many hats does he have now?

Fill in the bubble for the correct answer.

1. What is the total value of the coins?

○ 6¢

○ 15¢

○ 5¢

2. What is the total value of the coins?

○ 4¢

○ 12¢

○ 20¢

3. What is the value of a dime?

○ 5¢   ○ 1¢   ○ 10¢

GO ON

4. Which coin has a value of 25¢?

　○　　○　　○

---

5. How many pennies have the same value as a nickel?

○ 10　　　　○ 5　　　　○ 1

---

6. Angel has 8 pennies. He counts the pennies by twos.

What is the total value of the coins?

○ 4¢

○ 9¢

○ 8¢

7. Emily has 12 pennies. She counts the pennies by twos.

What is the total value of the coins?

    ○ 12¢   ○ 6¢   ○ 10¢

8. Max made 5 groups of pennies. He put 2 pennies in each group. What is the total value of the coins?

    ○ 10¢   ○ 5¢   ○ 7¢

9. Pia has 1 dime. Which group of coins shows the same amount in a different way?

   ○      ○   ○

GO ON ➤

10. Dev has 3 dimes. Which group of nickels shows the same amount in a different way?

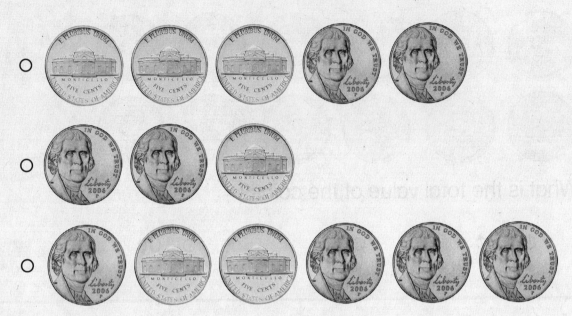

11. Liza counted 4 dimes by tens. How much money does she have?

   ○ 40¢

   ○ 4¢

   ○ 20¢

12. Amir has 6 nickels. Which shows the same amount in a different way?

○    ○   ○

Fill in the bubble for the correct answer.

1. Which way shows how to make a ten
   to solve 7 + 5?

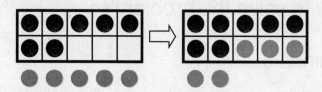

○ 7 + 7 + 2   ○ 7 + 3 + 2   ○ 7 + 3

---

2. Which shows a way to make a ten to subtract?

14 − 9

○ 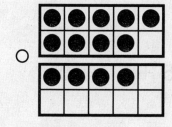   ○ 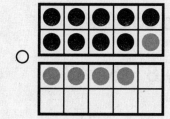   ○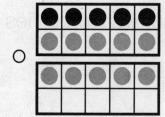

---

3. A squirrel has 17 acorns. Which
   subtraction sentence shows how to
   subtract 8 by making a ten?

○ 17 − 7 − 1 = 9

○ 17 − 10 = 7

○ 17 − 8 = 9

GO ON

4. There are 9 cars on a toy train. Parker joins 6 more cars to the train. How many cars are on the train now?

   Which tells how to solve the problem?

   ○ Subtract 9 minus 6.

   ○ Subtract 6.

   ○ Add $9 + 1 + 5$.

5. Eva eats 5 strawberries. Then she eats 8 more.

   Which number sentence shows how many strawberries Eva eats?

   ○ $5 + 8 = 13$ ○ $8 - 5 = 3$ ○ $5 + 5 = 10$

6. There are 7 birds in a tree. 6 more birds land in the tree. Then 5 birds fly away. How many birds are in the tree now?

   Which tells how to solve the problem?

   ○ Add 7 and 6.

   ○ Add 5 and 6. Subtract 7.

   ○ Add 7 and 6. Subtract 5.

7. Which subtraction fact matches the drawing?

    ○ $12 - 4 = 8$

    ○ $4 + 4 = 8$

    ○ $8 - 4 = 4$

---

8. Jin has 10 blocks. 2 are blue.
The rest are green.

Which number sentence shows how many
blocks are green?

    ○ $10 - 6 = 4$ ○ $10 - 2 = 8$ ○ $10 + 2 = 12$

---

9. Which story problem matches the addition
sentence $6 + 7 = 13$?

    ○ Sofia has 7 puzzles. Diego has 6 fewer puzzles
      than Sofia. How many puzzles do they have?

    ○ Sofia has 7 puzzles. She gives away 6 puzzles.
      How many puzzles does she have now?

    ○ Sofia has 6 puzzles. She buys 7 more puzzles.
      How many puzzles does she have?

GO ON

10. Which story problem matches the subtraction
sentence $15 - 8 = 7$?

○ Alex has 8 books. He gives 7 books to Julia.
How many books does Alex have now?

○ Alex has 15 books. He gives some away.
Then he has 7 books. How many books
does Alex give away?

○ Alex has 8 books. He buys 7 more books.
How many books does he have now?

---

11. Which addition sentence is shown?

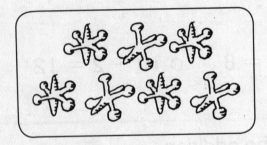 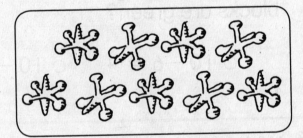

○ $6 + 10 = 16$ ○ $9 + 3 = 12$ ○ $7 + 9 = 16$

---

12. Which subtraction sentence is shown?

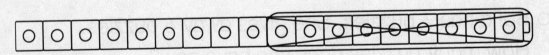

○ $16 - 8 = 8$ ○ $18 - 10 = 8$ ○ $18 - 9 = 9$

GO ON

13. Which coin has a value of 25¢?

  ○    ○    ○

---

14. How many dimes have the same value
as 4 nickels?

○ 2

○ 4

○ 1

---

15. What is the value of the coin?

○ 10¢

○ 1¢

○ 5¢

GO ON ▶

16. Layla has 10 pennies. She counts the pennies by twos.

What is the total value of the coins?

○ 5¢   ○ 9¢   ○ 10¢

17. Ari has 2 nickels. How many dimes have the same value as 2 nickels?

○ 1 dime

○ 2 dimes

○ 3 dimes

18. Ella has 20 pennies. How many dimes have the same value as 20 pennies?

○ 1 dime

○ 2 dimes

○ 3 dimes

Fill in the bubble for the correct answer.

I. Count forward.

98, 99, 100, ▢, ▢, ▢, ▢

What numbers come next?

○ 1, 2, 3, 4

○ 101, 102, 103, 104

○ 111, 112, 113, 114

---

2. Count backward.

75, 74, 73, ▢, ▢, ▢, ▢

What numbers come next?

○ 72, 71, 70, 69   ○ 74, 75, 76, 77   ○ 70, 69, 68, 67

---

3. Billy put the mittens in pairs.

Which shows how to count the mittens by twos?

○ 1, 2, 3, 4, 5

○ 2, 4, 6, 8, 10, 12, 14

○ 2, 4, 6, 8, 10

GO ON →

4. What number comes after 98 when skip counting by twos?

○ 100

○ 99

○ 102

5. Each star has 5 points.

How many points do all the stars have?
Skip count by 5s.

○ 60   ○ 65   ○ 13

6. There are 5 toes on each foot.

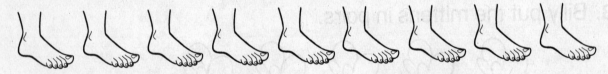

Which shows how to count the toes by fives?

○ 1, 2, 3, 4, 5, 6, 7, 8, 9

○ 10, 20, 30, 40, 50, 60, 70, 80, 90

○ 5, 10, 15, 20, 25, 30, 35, 40, 45

GO ON ➡

7. Anna put the marbles in groups of 10.

Which shows how to count the marbles by tens?

○ 1, 2, 3, 4, 5, 6

○ 5, 10, 15, 20, 25, 30

○ 10, 20, 30, 40, 50, 60

---

8. There are 10 markers in each box.

How many markers are in these boxes?
Skip count by 10s.

    ○ 11   ○ 110   ○ 100

---

9. Count by tens. What numbers are missing?

        77, 87, ▨ , ▨ , 117

○ 88, 89

○ 97, 107

○ 90, 100

GO ON ➡

10. Dan has 54 stickers. He buys 10 more.
Count forward by tens. How many stickers
does Dan have?

   ○ 64

   ○ 55

   ○ 56

11. Look at the chart. What are the
missing numbers?

10 Less	Number	10 More
	103	

   ○ 102 and 104

   ○ 93 and 104

   ○ 93 and 113

12. What number is 10 less than 119?

   ○ 109

   ○ 120

   ○ 118

Fill in the bubble for the correct answer.

1. Bo has 5 crayons. Pablo has 10 crayons.
How many more crayons does Pablo
have than Bo?

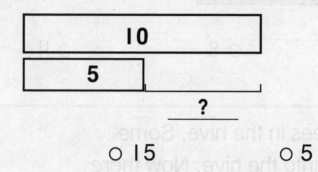

○ 6   ○ 15   ○ 5

---

2. Callie has 8 pins. Adam has 6 pins. How many
fewer pins does Adam have than Callie?

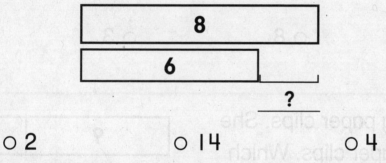

○ 2   ○ 14   ○ 4

---

3. There are 9 bugs on a leaf. Then 3 more bugs
land on the leaf. How many bugs are on the leaf?

[image: row of squares, 9 white squares then 3 shaded squares]

○ 6   ○ 11   ○ 12

GO ON

4. Mel sees 4 chipmunks on the deck.
Then 4 more chipmunks join them. How
many chipmunks are on the deck?

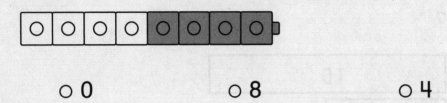

    ○ 0   ○ 8   ○ 4

---

5. There are 5 bees in the hive. Some
more bees fly into the hive. Now there
are 13 bees in the hive. How many bees
fly into the hive?

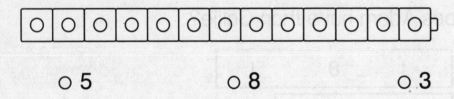

    ○ 5   ○ 8   ○ 3

---

6. Gina has 9 big paper clips. She
has 6 small paper clips. Which
number sentence shows how
many paper clips Gina has?

9	6

?

○ $9 + 6 = 15$

○ $9 - 6 = 3$

○ $6 + 3 = 9$

GO ON

7. There are 11 petals on the flower. Some petals fall off. Now there are 8 petals. How many petals fall off?

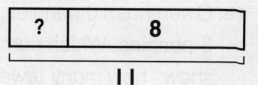

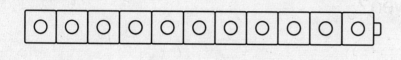

○ 4   ○ 8   ○ 3

---

8. There are 9 peppers. 7 peppers are red. The rest are green. How many peppers are green?

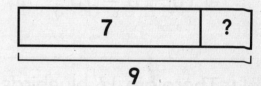

○ 2   ○ 16   ○ 8

---

9. Luke has 14 pretzels. Kim has 5 pretzels. How many more pretzels does Luke have than Kim?

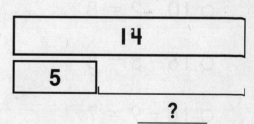

○ 5

○ 9

○ 7

GO ON ➡

10. Owen has 10 pennies. Tamar has 3 pennies. Which number sentence shows how many fewer pennies Tamar has than Owen?

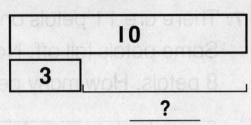

○ $10 - 3 = 7$

○ $7 - 3 = 4$

○ $10 + 3 = 13$

11. There are 16 bluebirds on a fence. There are 8 robins. Which number sentence shows how many more bluebirds than robins are on the fence?

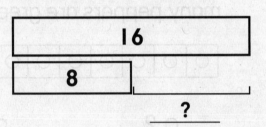

○ $10 - 2 = 8$

○ $16 - 8 = 8$

○ $16 - 9 = 7$

12. Jack has 7 books. He buys some more. Now he has 15 books. How many books does Jack buy?

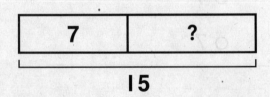

○ 7   ○ 9   ○ 8

STOP

Fill in the bubble for the correct answer.

1. What is the sum for $8 + 2 + 4$?

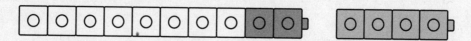

○ 6　　　　　　　○ 12　　　　　　　○ 14

---

2. Which model does **NOT** show a way to add $3 + 7 + 1$?

○

○

○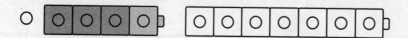

---

3. Which model shows a way to find the sum for $1 + 3 + 6$?

○

○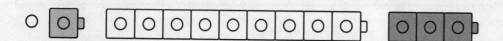

○

GO ON →

4. What is the sum of 8 + 3 + 5?

○ 11

○ 16

○ 8

---

5. Which is **NOT** a way to add 2 + 6 + 2?

○ 2 + 2 = 4; 4 + 6 = 10

○ 2 + 6 = 8; 8 + 2 = 10

○ 2 + 2 = 4; 2 + 6 = 8

---

6. A rabbit eats 4 carrots on Monday.
It eats 6 carrots on Tuesday. It eats
3 carrots on Wednesday. How many
carrots does the rabbit eat?

○ 13

○ 10

○ 14

Name _____

7. Alonzo scores 9 points in a soccer game.
Dylan scores 1 point. Molly scores 5 points.
How many points do they score?

○ 15

○ 14

○ 10

---

8. Which shows the same addends in a
different order?

$$9$$
$$+\ 5$$
$$\overline{14}$$

○ $\begin{array}{r} 4 \\ +\ 5 \\ \hline 9 \end{array}$ ○ $\begin{array}{r} 5 \\ +\ 9 \\ \hline 14 \end{array}$ ○ $\begin{array}{r} 8 \\ +\ 6 \\ \hline 14 \end{array}$

---

9. Which shows the same addends in a
different order?

$$6 + 7 = 13$$

○ $6 + 7 = 13$ ○ $8 + 5 = 13$ ○ $7 + 6 = 13$

GO ON

10. Which is the sum for $8 + 3 + 7$?

    ○ 15

    ○ 11

    ○ 18

---

11. Leah has 6 roses, 6 daisies, and 3 tulips.
How many flowers does Leah have?

    ○ 15

    ○ 12

    ○ 14

---

12. Jamal sees 2 sailboats. He sees 3 kayaks.
He sees 6 motorboats. Which shows
how many boats he sees in all?

    ○ 8

    ○ 11

    ○ 9

(STOP)

Fill in the bubble for the correct answer.

1. What number would make expressions of equal value?

$$17 - 8 = 2 + \blacksquare$$

- ○ 9
- ○ 7
- ○ 15

---

2. What number completes the related facts?

$14 - \blacksquare = 8$ $\blacksquare + 8 = 14$

$14 - 8 = \blacksquare$ $8 + \blacksquare = 14$

- ○ 8
- ○ 6
- ○ 14

---

3. What number completes the related fact?

$$5 + 7 = 12 \text{ and } \blacksquare - 7 = 5$$

- ○ 12
- ○ 2
- ○ 11

GO ON

4. What is the unknown number?

$$9 + \blacksquare = 13 \quad 13 - 9 = \blacksquare$$

○ 9

○ 5

○ 4

5. Which addition sentence can you use to check the subtraction?

$$18 - 9 = \blacksquare$$

○ $9 + 9 = 18$

○ $7 + 9 = 16$

○ $9 + 2 = 11$

6. Which addition fact helps you solve $11 - 3$?

○ $3 + 5 = 8$

○ $9 + 1 = 10$

○ $8 + 3 = 11$

GO ON ➡

7. Which completes the related facts?

$$7 + 8 = 15 \qquad 15 - 8 = 7$$
$$8 + 7 = 15 \qquad \underline{\quad ? \quad}$$

○ $15 - 9 = 6$

○ $15 - 7 = 8$

○ $8 - 7 = 1$

---

8. Which subtraction fact is related to
$5 + 8 = 13$?

○ $13 - 8 = 5$

○ $8 - 5 = 3$

○ $13 - 9 = 4$

---

9. There are 16 children in the park. Then
7 children go home. Which addition sentence
can you use to check the subtraction?

○ $5 + 9 = 14$

○ $7 + 5 = 12$

○ $7 + 9 = 16$

10. What is the unknown number?

$$\blacksquare + 8 = 17 \quad 17 - \blacksquare = 8$$

○ 8

○ 17

○ 9

---

11. Reed has 13 cubes. 6 cubes are red.
4 cubes are green. The rest are blue.
How many cubes are blue?

○ 3

○ 10

○ 19

---

12. Which addition fact helps you solve $15 - 6$?

○ $4 + 2 = 6$

○ $9 + 6 = 15$

○ $5 + 6 = 11$

Fill in the bubble for the correct answer.

1. Jenna has 5 bows. Asia has 8 bows. How many fewer bows does Jenna have than Asia?

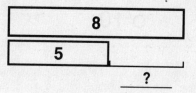

- ○ 13
- ○ 3
- ○ 2

2. What is the sum of 4 + 6 + 2?

- ○ 10
- ○ 11
- ○ 12

3. Which model does **NOT** show a way to add 9 + 5 + 1?

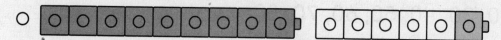

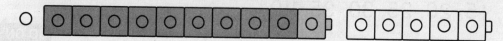

GO ON ➡

4. What is the sum of $5 + 2 + 8$?

　　　○ 10　　　　　○ 13　　　　　○ 15

---

5. Each hand has 5 fingers.

How many fingers are on all of the hands?
Skip count by 5s.

　　○ 12

　　○ 60

　　○ 55

---

6. Colin put 10 paper clips in each bag.

Which shows how to count the paper
clips by tens?

　　○ 1, 2, 3, 4, 5, 6, 7, 8

　　○ 10, 20, 30, 40, 50, 60, 70, 80

　　○ 5, 10, 15, 20, 25, 30, 35, 40

GO ON ➡

7. Look at the chart. What are the missing numbers?

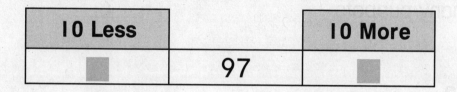

10 Less		10 More
⬜	97	⬜

○ 87 and 107   ○ 96 and 98   ○ 90 and 100

---

8. There are 9 fish in the reef. Then 1 more fish joins them. How many fish are in the reef now?

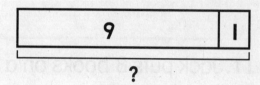

9	1
?	

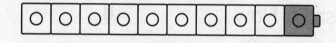

○ 8   ○ 11   ○ 10

---

9. Aliya has 3 pens. Then she buys some more pens. Now she has 12 pens. How many pens does she buy?

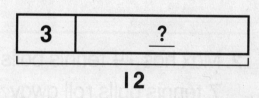

3	?
12	

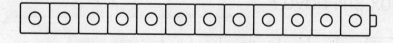

○ 8   ○ 9   ○ 10

GO ON ➡

10. Darryl has 5 puppets. Lucia has 7 puppets. Which number sentence shows how many puppets they have?

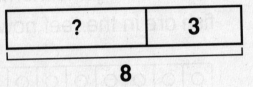

○ 5 + 7 = 12

○ 7 − 5 = 2

○ 5 + 2 = 7

---

11. Jack puts 8 books on a shelf. Then he gives away some books. Now there are 3 books on the shelf. How many books does Jack give away?

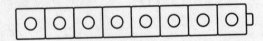

○ 5   ○ 11   ○ 8

---

12. Max has 14 tennis balls. Then 7 tennis balls roll away. How many tennis balls does Max still have?

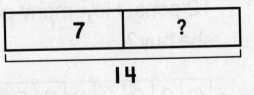

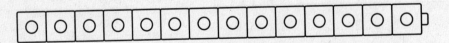

○ 4   ○ 9   ○ 7

GO ON ➡

13. Some children were on the swings. 2 children went home. Then there were 8 children. Which number sentence shows how many children were on the swings to start?

2	8

?

○ $8 - 2 = 6$

○ $2 + 8 = 10$

○ $10 - 5 = 5$

14. Tomoko has 9 pennies. Bart has 7 pennies. Which number sentence shows how many fewer pennies Bart has than Tomoko?

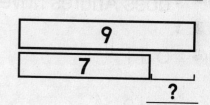

?

○ $9 + 7 = 16$

○ $8 - 6 = 2$

○ $9 - 7 = 2$

15. What number would make expressions of equal value?

$$18 - 9 = 6 + \blacksquare$$

○ 9   ○ 3   ○ 15

GO ON →

16. What number completes the related facts?

$$15 - \blacksquare = 9 \qquad \blacksquare + 9 = 15$$

$$15 - 9 = \blacksquare \qquad 9 + \blacksquare = 15$$

     ○ 15   ○ 5   ○ 6

---

17. Andrés has 4 red trains, 3 blue trains,
     and 4 yellow trains. How many trains
     does Andrés have?

     ○ 11

     ○ 12

     ○ 8

---

18. Which addition fact helps you solve
     $\blacksquare = 17 - 8$?

     ○ $7 + 8 = 15$

     ○ $8 + 9 = 17$

     ○ $5 + 5 = 10$

Name ____________________

Fill in the bubble for the correct answer.

1. Which two shapes make a circle?

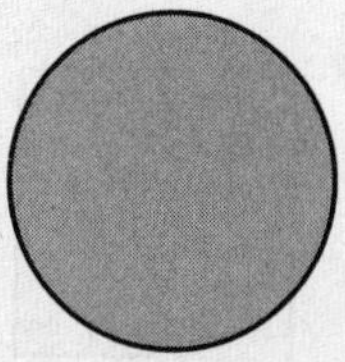

○ 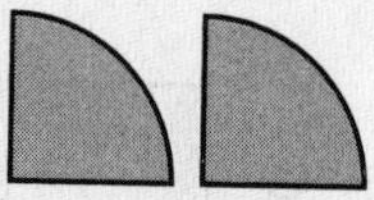   ○ 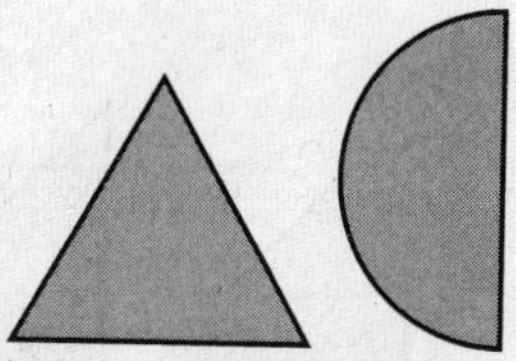   ○ 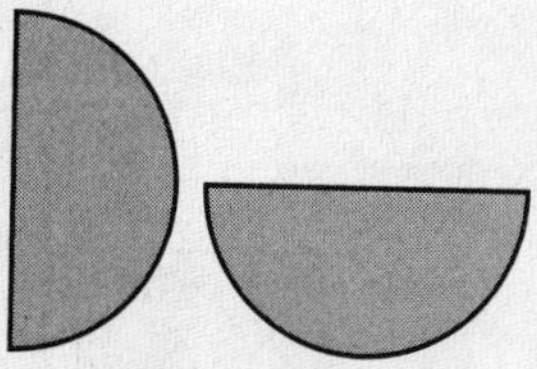

---

2. Which two shapes make a triangle?

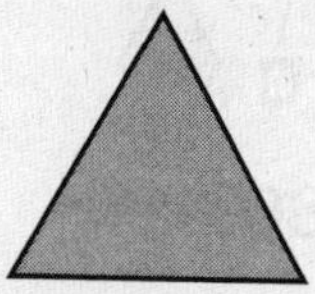

○ 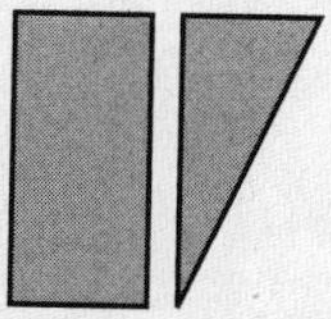   ○ 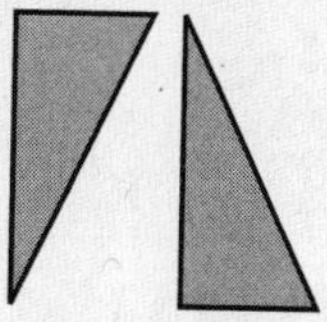   ○ 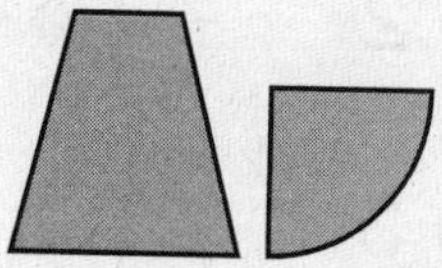

---

3. Which new shape can be made?

Step 1: Combine 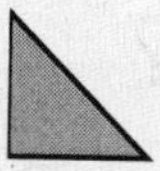 and 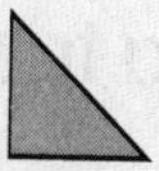 to make .

Step 2: Then use  and .

○ 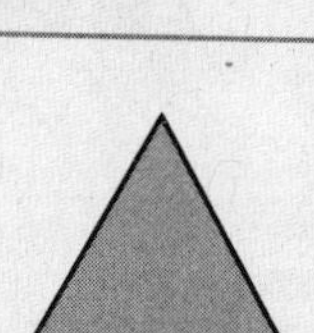   ○ 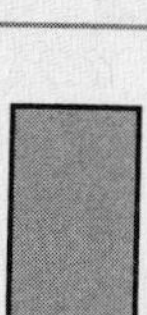   ○ 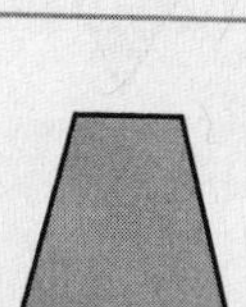

GO ON

4. Which two shapes do **NOT** make a square?

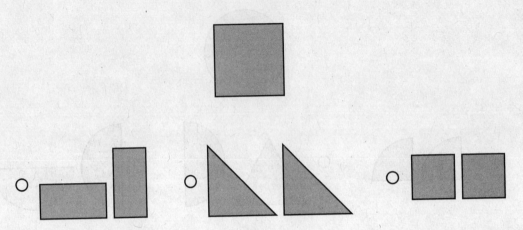

○   ○   ○

---

5. Alberto uses △ to make a ◇.
How many △ does he use?

○ 2

○ 3

○ 4

---

6. Which shape is **NOT** a triangle?

 ○    ○   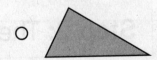 ○

GO ON ➡

Name _____

7. Mendy draws a shape with 4 straight sides and 4 vertices. All the sides are the same length. Which shape does he draw?

○ triangle

○ square

○ circle

8. Circles are curved and closed shapes.

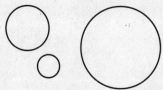

Which shape would be sorted into this group?

  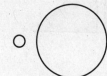

9. Dara draws a shape with 4 straight sides and 4 vertices. Which shape might she draw?

○ rectangle

○ triangle

○ circle

GO ON

10. How many straight sides does a hexagon have?

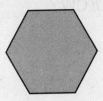

○ 6   ○ 5   ○ 4

---

11. Which shapes can combine to make this shape?

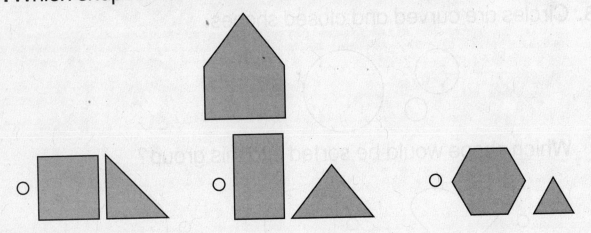

○   ○   ○

---

12. Hattie makes this shape with blocks.

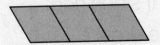

She makes a different shape with the same
blocks. Which shape can she make?

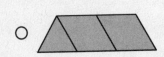   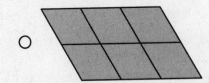   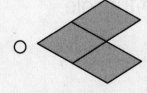

○   ○   ○

Fill in the bubble for the correct answer.

1. Janya has a mystery shape. How can she describe the shape so you know it is a three-dimensional solid?

   ○ big and green

   ○ 5 faces, 9 edges, 6 vertices

   ○ small and pointy

2. Wyatt has a mystery shape. Which clue would **NOT** help you guess the shape?

   ○ small

   ○ 1 flat surface

   ○ can roll

3. Carlos buys a toy for his friend. The bottom of the toy looks like this.

   Which could **NOT** be the shape of the toy?

   ○ 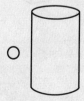   ○   ○

GO ON

4. Which solid is a sphere?

○   ○   ○

---

5. Which solid is a cone?

○   ○   ○

---

6. Which solid is a triangular prism?

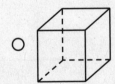   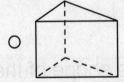   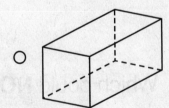

○   ○   ○

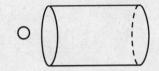

GO ON

7. Milo has a ball. It is shaped like a sphere.
How many flat surfaces does a sphere have?

   ○ 2

   ○ 1

   ○ 0

---

8. Which solid has both flat and curved surfaces?

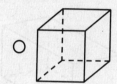 ○   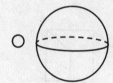 ○   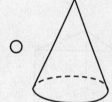 ○

---

9. Nia has a block that is shaped like a cylinder.
How many flat surfaces does the block have?

   ○ 2

   ○ 6

   ○ 1

GO ON →

10. Which solid has 6 faces, 12 edges, and
    8 vertices?

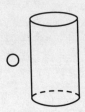 ○   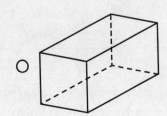 ○   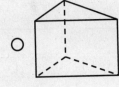 ○

---

11. David has a solid in a bag. It has 6 faces.
    All the faces are squares of the same size.
    Which solid could be in David's bag?

○ 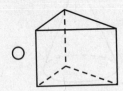   ○ 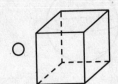   ○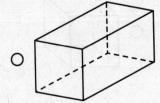

---

12. Julia has rectangular prisms, cubes, and
    triangular prisms. She sorts them by the
    number of edges. Which is the only
    solid with 9 edges?

○ 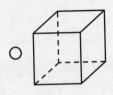   ○ 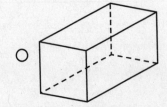   ○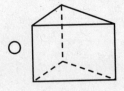

STOP

Fill in the bubble for the correct answer.

1. Which does **NOT** show 2 equal parts?

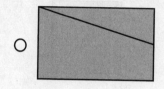 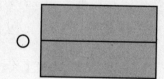 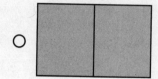

2. Which triangle shows 2 equal shares?

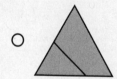 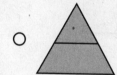 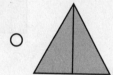

3. Kathryn is cutting circles into 2 equal parts.
   Which circle shows halves?

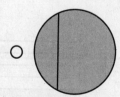 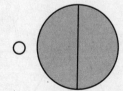 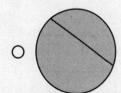

GO ON

4. Which shape shows 4 equal shares?

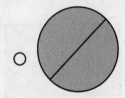 ○   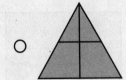 ○   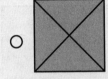 ○

5. Arun cuts a rectangle into 4 equal shares. Which is **NOT** a name for one of the fair shares?

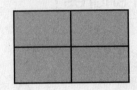

○ a fourth

○ a half

○ a quarter

6. Which shows a fourth of the shape shaded?

○ 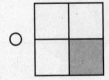   ○    ○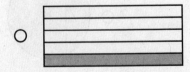

GO ON ➡

7. James has a pie. He shares an equal part
with his friend. Which shows halves?

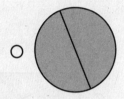 ○   ○ 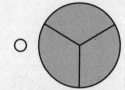   ○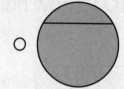

8. Which shape shows fourths?

○ 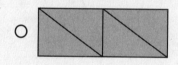   ○ 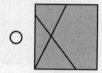   ○

9. Which shape does **NOT** show halves?

○ 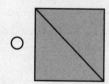   ○ 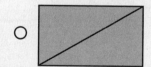   ○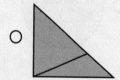

GO ON ➡

10. Sofia cuts a granola bar into two equal parts to share with her friend. Which does **NOT** show halves?

○ 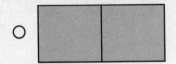   ○ 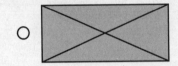   ○

11. Which shape does **NOT** show fourths?

○ 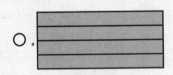   ○    ○

12. Tim has a pizza. He cuts it into 4 equal parts. Which does **NOT** show fourths?

○ 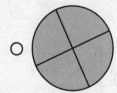   ○ 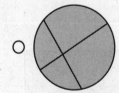   ○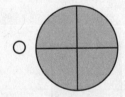

STOP

Fill in the bubble for the correct answer.

1. A box is the same length as this string.
Which object will fit in the box?

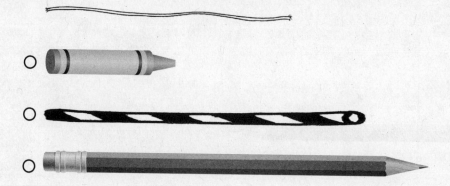

○ (crayon)

○ (straw)

○ (pencil)

---

2. Swati measures this marker with .
About how long is the marker?

○ about 5 ▮

○ about 4 ▮

○ about 14 ▮

---

3. Eli uses 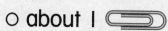 to measure his phone.
About how long is the phone?

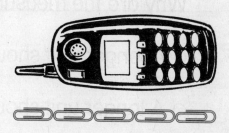

○ about 1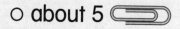

○ about 3 ▭

○ about 5 ▭

GO ON ➡

4. Rae measures a book with different units. Which unit would she use the most of?

○

○

○

5. Mark measures from the TV to the couch. The distance is 60 . Which unit will measure the same distance with the fewest units?

○ ●   ○ 🗝   ○

6. A brush is about 8 🪙 long. Mira measures the same brush and finds it is 2 ✏️ long. Why are the measurements different?

○ A longer unit should use fewer units.

○ A longer unit should use more units.

○ An object cannot be measured with different units.

GO ON ➡️

7. Dan measures his arm with different units. Which unit will he use the most of?

○ [cube]

○ [pencil]

○ [crayon]

8. Suzy measures from her desk to the door. The distance is 17 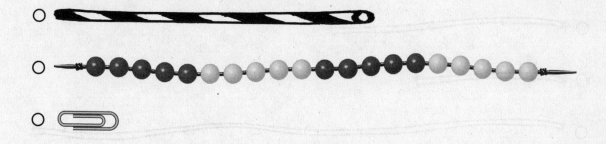. Which of these units would she need more of to measure that distance?

○ [straw]

○ [beaded string]

○ [paper clip]

9. Matt measures a toy truck with different units. Which unit would he use the fewest of?

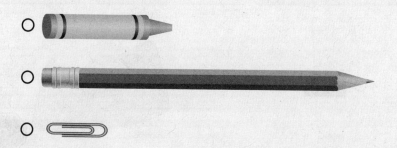

○ [crayon]

○ [pencil]

○ [paper clip]

GO ON

10. Which writing utensil is about 2 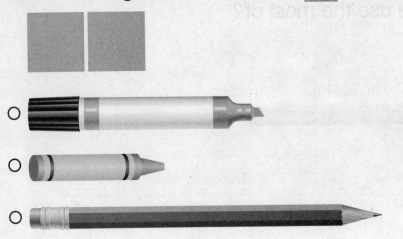 long?

○

○

○

---

11. Which piece of yarn is about 4 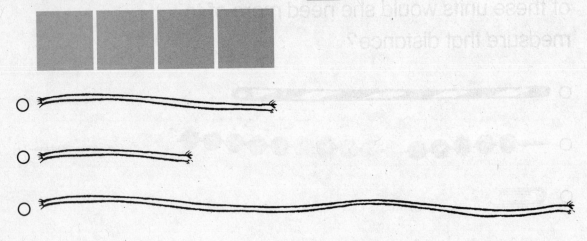 long?

○

○

○

---

12. Which real object is about 7  long?

○    ○   ○

Fill in the bubble for the correct answer.

1. Anna finishes her homework at 6 o'clock.
Which clock shows that time?

○    ○    ○

---

2. What time is it?

○ 7:00   ○ 8:00   ○ 6 o'clock

---

3. On Liam's clock the hour hand points to the 4.
Which is Liam's clock?

○    ○    ○

GO ON ➡

4. What time does the clock show?

○ 12:00   ○ 1:00   ○ 2:00

---

5. The clock shows the time that David starts science class. What time does the clock show?

○ 10:00   ○ 12:00   ○ 11:00

---

6. What time does the clock show?

○ 8 o'clock   ○ 10 o'clock   ○ 9 o'clock

GO ON

7. Mary Ann eats dinner at the time on the clock.
What time does the clock show?

○ half past 7   ○ half past 6   ○ half past 5

8. Which clock shows half past 11?

○    ○    ○

9. What is the time?

○ half past 2   ○ 2:00   ○ 6 o'clock

GO ON

Name _____

10. What time does the clock show?

○  1:00   ○ 1:30   ○ 2:30

---

11. The clock shows the time that Terry goes
to bed. What time does the clock show?

○  8:00   ○  9:30   ○  8:30

---

12. What time does the clock show?

 12:30

○    ○    ○

Fill in the bubble for the correct answer.

1. Zoe uses 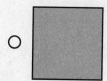 to make a ◆.

   How many does she use?

   ○ 4

   ○ 3

   ○ 2

---

2. Which shape is a square?

    ○   ○    ○

---

3. How many straight sides does a
   triangle have?

   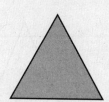

   ○ 4   ○ 3   ○ 5

GO ON ➡

4. Henry draws a shape with 4 straight sides and 4 vertices. Which shape does he draw?

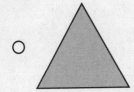 ○   ○ 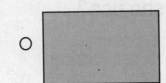   ○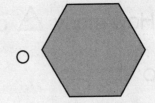

5. Lourdes has a sphere. It has only a curved surface. How many flat surfaces does it have?

○ 0

○ 2

○ I

6. Which solid has a curved surface and only I flat surface?

○ 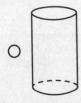   ○ 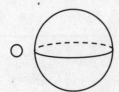   ○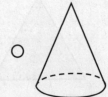

GO ON

7. Tim has a toy that is shaped like a cylinder.
How many flat surfaces does it have?

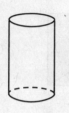

○ 3   ○ I   ○ 2

8. Jill makes this shape with blocks.

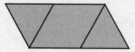

Which blocks does she use?

      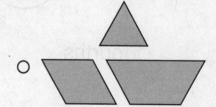

9. Noah is cutting shapes into 2 equal shares.
Which shows halves?

○   ○ 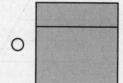   ○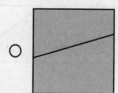

GO ON

10. Ping is cutting rectangles into 2 equal parts.
    Which rectangle shows halves?

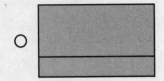 ○ 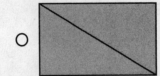 ○ 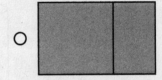 ○

11. Carlos cuts a circle into 4 equal shares.
    Which is **NOT** a name for the shares?

○ fourths   ○ halves   ○ quarters

12. Lucy cuts a shape into 4 equal parts.
    Which shape shows 1 equal part shaded?

○ 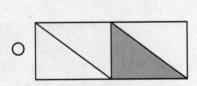   ○ 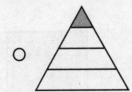   ○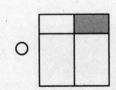

GO ON ▶

13. Which shape does **NOT** show fourths?

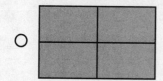   ○   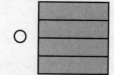   ○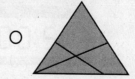

14. Zion measures from the table to the sink.
Which unit will measure the length with
the fewest units?

○

○ (thumbtack)

○ (bead)

15. What time is it?

○ 3:00

○ 10 o'clock

○ 9:00

GO ON ▶

16. What time does the clock show?

○ 2 o'clock   ○ 12 o'clock   ○ 11 o'clock

---

17. Chloe gets home at the time on the clock.
    What time does the clock show?

○ half past 5   ○ half past 3   ○ half past 4

---

18. What time does the clock show?

○ 7:30   ○ 7:00   ○ 8:30

STOP

Name _____

Fill in the bubble for the correct answer.

1. Are there more boys or girls in the class?
Jada makes 1 tally mark for each child.
Which could be her tally chart?

○
Boys and Girls in Class		Total
boys	IIII	4
girls	IIII III	8

○
Our Eye Color		Total
black	IIII	5
blue	IIII III	8
brown	IIII II	7

○
Apple Colors		Total
red	IIII I	6
green	IIII	5

2. Bryan has a box of crayons. He sorts them
by color. He tallies to record. Which could
be his tally chart?

○
Crayons in a Box		Total
red	I	1
yellow	IIII	5
blue	IIII	4

○
Crayons in a Box		Total
big	IIII II	7
little	III	3

○
Writing Tools		Total
crayons	II	2
markers	IIII III	8
pencils	III	3

3. Which tally chart shows how many
pieces of fruit are in the bowl?

○
Fruit in the Bowl		Total
bananas	IIII I	6
apples	III	3
berries	III	3

○
Fruit in the Bowl		Total
bananas	I	1
apples	III	3
berries	III	3

○
Fruit in the Bowl		Total
lemons	II	2
limes	IIII	4
oranges	III	3

4. Nami makes a T-chart. It shows each child's choice for favorite dinner. Pizza wins! Which could be her T-chart?

○ | pizza | pasta |
|---|---|
| IIII | HH III |

○ | pizza | pasta |
|---|---|
| II | HH I |

○ | pizza | pasta |
|---|---|
| HH III | IIII |

5. John asks 10 children which snack they like better. This is what he found.

Popcorn or Chips?	
Jim: popcorn	Eva: chips
Lin: chips	Ruby: popcorn
Dyanna: chips	Emilio: chips
Will: chips	Peyton: popcorn
Hayley: chips	Anthony: chips

Which shows a T-chart for this data?

○ | popcorn | chips |
|---|---|
| HH II | III |

○ | popcorn | chips |
|---|---|
| III | HH II |

○ | popcorn | chips |
|---|---|
| IIII | HH I |

6. Malia asks 10 children which color they like better. Each child chooses blue or yellow. Which could be her T-chart?

○ | blue | yellow |
|---|---|
| HH | I |

○ | red | green |
|---|---|
| II | III |

○ | blue | yellow |
|---|---|
| HH I | IIII |

GO ON

7. Sam asks classmates to tell whether
they like soccer or baseball better.
He made this T-chart.

soccer	baseball
HHI	III

How many children chose soccer?

○ 5   ○ 4   ○ 3

8. How many more children chose
movies than books?

books	movies
HHI I	HHI III

○ 6   ○ 2   ○ 8

9. Luna drew O for each child's choice.
2 children chose dogs. 8 children chose cats.
Which could be Luna's picture graph?

○
Our Favorite Pet		
dogs	O O	
cats	O O	

○
Our Favorite Pet		
dogs	O O O O O O O O O	
cats	O O O O O	

○
Our Favorite Pet		
dogs	O O	
cats	O O O O O O O O	

GO ON ▶

10. Which would be a good title for the bar graph?

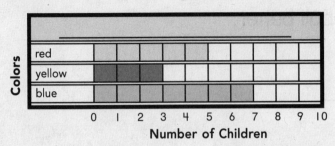

○ Books We Read   ○ Favorite Color   ○ Hours of Sleep

---

11. Look at the picture graph.
Who has the most stuffed animals?

Stuffed Animals We Have								
Sophie	☆	☆	☆	☆	☆	☆	☆	☆
Carter	☆	☆	☆	☆	☆			
Avery	☆	☆	☆					

Each ☆ stands for 1 stuffed animal.

○ Avery   ○ Carter   ○ Sophie

---

12. Which question could be answered by looking
at the picture graph?

Our Favorite Gadget								
computer	○	○	○	○	○	○	○	○
television	○	○	○					

Each ○ stands for 1 child.

○ How many children chose the computer?

○ Which fruit did more children choose?

○ How many children chose red and blue?

13. How many children chose grapes?

Our Favorite Fruit								
grapes	웃	웃	웃	웃	웃			
apples	웃	웃	웃	웃	웃	웃	웃	

Each 웃 stands for 1 child.

○ 5 children   ○ 7 children   ○ 2 children

Use the bar graph for 14–15.

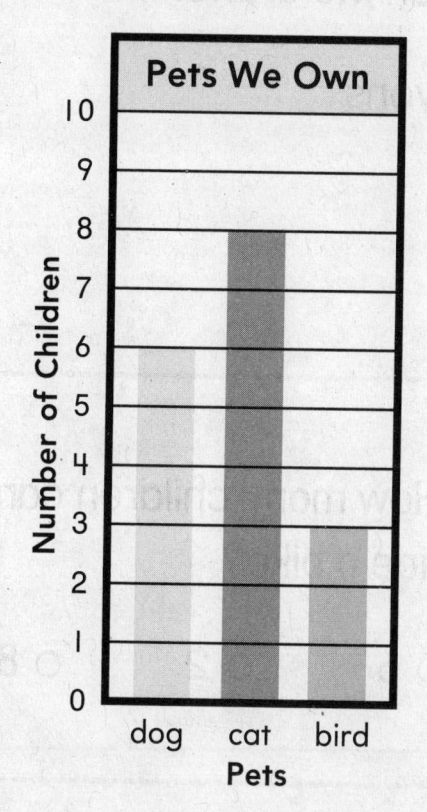

14. Which pet is owned by the most children?

○ bird

○ dog

○ cat

15. Which pet is owned by the fewest children?

○ cat

○ dog

○ bird

GO ON

16. Jake made this bar graph.

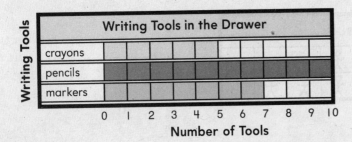

Which question could be answered
by looking at the bar graph?

○ How many hours did it take to clean the drawer?

○ How many more pencils than crayons
are in the drawer?

○ How many children chose pens?

Use the bar graph for 17–18.

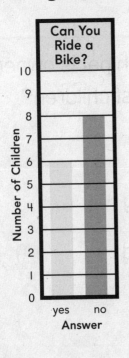

17. How many children can
ride a bike?

○ 6   ○ 2   ○ 8

18. How many children
answered the question?

○ 13   ○ 14   ○ 2

Fill in the bubble for the correct answer.

1. Audrey earns 10¢ each time she takes out the garbage. What does Audrey earn for taking out the garbage 5 times?

○ 50¢

○ 5¢

○ 15¢

2. Logan sells bookmarks at the craft fair for 5¢ each. What does Logan earn for selling 3 bookmarks?

○ 8¢

○ 15¢

○ 53¢

3. Kalini earns 25¢ for each hour she washes cars. What does Kalini earn for washing cars for 2 hours?

○ 23¢

○ 27¢

○ 50¢

GO ON

4. Bob buys two of these things to bake a cake. Which thing might he want but not need?

 ○    ○    ○

5. Tina is a fire fighter. She needs two of these things to do her job. Which thing might she want but not need?

○    ○    ○

6. Luis is going to the beach.

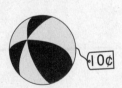      

What is the total cost of the two things above that he will need for the beach?

○ 60¢   ○ 59¢   ○ 19¢

GO ON ➡

7. Elise is going to school.

What is the total cost of the two things above that she will need at school?

○ 37¢   ○ 27¢   ○ 50¢

8. Mr. Brown is a farmer. He uses his income to buy goods and services. Which goods might he buy?

○ a visit to a dentist to fill a cavity

○ food for animals and seeds for crops

○ a visit from a plumber to fix drips in the sink

9. Mrs. Brown is a teacher. She uses her income to pay for goods and services. Which service might she buy?

○ haircut

○ shoes

○ a dress

GO ON

10. Zander buys a newspaper for 10¢. Which word tells what he does with the money?

   ○ spend

   ○ save

   ○ invest

11. Felix spends 5¢ each day on milk. How much money does Felix spend in 5 days?

   ○ 20¢

   ○ 10¢

   ○ 25¢

12. Lashawna has 18¢. She spends 9¢ to buy an apple. How much money does Lashawna have left?

   ○ 9¢

   ○ 27¢

   ○ 10¢

13. Elle gets 25¢ for allowance each week. She puts the money in a special box. Which word tells what she does with the money?

○ spend

○ buy

○ save

14. Atticus saves 5¢ each week for 3 weeks. How much money does Atticus save?

○ 8¢

○ 15¢

○ 10¢

15. Jamika saves 10¢ each week for 8 weeks. Then she spends 50¢ to buy a book. How much money does Jamika have left?

○ 30¢

○ 75¢

○ 80¢

GO ON

16. Gia puts these coins in the sharing jar.
She gives the money to others in need.

What is the total value of these coins?

○ 23¢   ○ 27¢   ○ 32¢

---

17. Asher puts money in the sharing jar. He
has 3 dimes, 2 nickels, and 8 pennies.
What is the total value of these coins?

○ 48¢

○ 58¢

○ 33¢

---

18. Markell puts these coins in the sharing jar.
He gives the money to others in need.

What is the total value of these coins?

○ 33¢   ○ 60¢   ○ 45¢

Child's Name _____ Date _____

Prerequisite Skills Inventory

Item	Grade K Lesson	Grade K TEKS*	Common Error	Intervene with RtI* Tier 1 Lessons	Soar to Success Math
1	2.4	K.2.A	May not know the numbers in counting order	1	1.03
2	2.4	K.2.A	May not understand how to count backward	1	1.03
3	6.4	K.2.F	May not understand the concept of one more	34	7.11, 7.12
4	6.4	K.2.F	May not understand the concept of one less	34	7.11, 7.12
5	6.6	K.2.H	May not understand the concepts of less than and greater than	41	7.09
6	8.8	K.2.H	May not understand the concepts of less than and greater than	42	70.01
7	9.4	K.2.I	May count all the cubes	46	10.03, 11.03
8	11.1	K.3.A	May count only the children on the swings	55	10.03, 10.04, 10.09
9	12.1	K.3.A	May count both of the frogs	56	11.03
10	15.4	K.4	May not be able to distinguish between quarters and other coins	76	27.05
11	16.1	K.5	May only look at the ones digit	78	28.10
12	16.3	K.5	May not count by tens	80	28.11, 28.12
13	17.4	K.6.A	May not recognize a square	85	38.02, 38.07
14	20.5	K.6.B	May not recognize an object shaped as a cube	100	53.06

*TEKS—Texas Essential Knowledge and Skills; RtI—Response to Intervention

Item	Grade K Lesson	Grade K TEKS*	Common Error	Intervene with RtI* Tier 1 Lessons	Soar to Success Math
15	18.5	K.6.C	May not recognize a flat surface on a cylinder	90	39.13, 39.26
16	17.2	K.6.D	May not know how many sides there are on a triangle	83	38.02, 38.07
17	18.3	K.6.E	May not be able to classify squares	88	39.13, 39.26
18	19.2	K.7.B	May not understand the meaning of *longer*	93	41.02
19	19.3	K.7.B	May not understand the meaning of *shorter*	94	41.03
20	19.4	K.7.B	May not understand the meaning of *lighter*	95	42.02
21	20.4	K.8.C	May not understand how to read a picture graph	99	53.06
22	21.1	K.9.A	May not understand the concept of earning money	97	38.04, 38.06, 38.05
23	21.2	K.9.B	May not be able to distinguish between earning money and getting money as a gift	97	38.04, 38.06, 38.05
24	21.4	K.9.C	May not recognize the skills needed to do a job	39	7.06
25	21.3	K.9.D	May not be able to distinguish between wants and needs	97	38.04, 38.06, 38.05

*TEKS—Texas Essential Knowledge and Skills; **RtI**—Response to Intervention

Child's Name _____ Date _____

Beginning-of-Year Test

Item	Lesson	TEKS*	Common Error	Intervene with RtI* Tier 1 Lessons	Soar to Success Math
1	1.4	1.2.B	May confuse the tens place and the ones place	4	1.14, 1.15
2	1.7	1.2.C	May not count all pieces in the model	7	2.20
3	2.4	1.2.D	May confuse greater than and less than	9	7.18
4	2.4	1.2.E	May not understand how to use place value to compare numbers	9	7.18
5	2.5	1.2.F	May confuse the meaning of least and greatest	10	35.10
6	2.1	1.2.G	May not know the difference between > and <	11	7.18
7	3.1	1.3.A	May not understand ten frames	14	10.15
8	4.1	1.3.B	May not understand that the picture represents addition	17	10.03
9	4.6	1.3.C	May not match the addends to the model	25	10.13
10	7.1	1.3.D	May add instead of subtracting	37	11.13
11	8.1	1.3.E	May think the problem shows subtraction	44	66.01
12	8.3	1.3.F	May not know the words to represent subtraction in a word problem	47	11.12
13	9.1	1.4.A	May confuse a dime with a nickel	48	3.09

*TEKS—Texas Essential Knowledge and Skills; RtI—Response to Intervention

Beginning-of-Year Test (continued)

Item	Lesson	TEKS*	Common Error	Intervene with RtI* Tier 1 Lessons	Soar to Success Math
14	9.4	1.4.C	May count the pennies in one row to find the total value	51	3.11
15	10.1	1.5.A	May count backward instead of forward	52	28.12
16	10.3	1.5.B	May count the pairs by ones instead of by twos	54	31.04
17	10.6	1.5.C	May count forward by ones instead of by tens	57	28.14
18	11.1	1.5.D	May subtract instead of adding	59	10.03
19	4.2	1.5.E	May not recognize that the sum must be greater than each addend	18	10.03, 10.09
20	12.1	1.5.F	May subtract instead of adding	64	10.08
21	13.2	1.5.G	May subtract a different number from 13	69	29.31
22	14.1	1.6.A	May not understand the term "vertices"	73	38.11
23	14.2	1.6.B	May think that color is a feature that defines a shape	74	38.12
24	14.1	1.6.D	May think the crescent is a circle since it is curved and closed	73	38.11
25	15.2	1.6.E	May not understand that a solid can have no flat surfaces	75	39.17, 39.26
26	14.4	1.6.F	May not be able to visualize which shapes compose a trapezoid	81	38.17
27	16.2	1.6.G	May think that any straight line divides a square into equal parts	82	5.03
28	16.3	1.6.H	May think that every shape with four parts shows fourths	84	5.05

*TEKS—Texas Essential Knowledge and Skills; **RtI**—Response to Intervention

Beginning-of-Year Test (continued)

Item	Lesson	TEKS*	Common Error	Intervene with RtI* Tier 1 Lessons	Soar to Success Math
29	17.1	1.7.A	May not use direct comparison to choose the answer	85	41.02
30	17.2	1.7.B	May have difficulty counting the number of tiles below the pencil	86	41.06
31	17.4	1.7.C	May think that a shorter unit would require fewer units to measure the distance	88	41.06
32	17.2	1.7.D	May think that 3 tiles is the shortest length	86	41.06
33	18.3	1.7.E	May not understand that "o'clock" can replace "00"	91	51.08, 51.10
34	19.5	1.8.A	May not understand that the number of tally marks should be greater for dogs than for cats	95	54.03
35	19.2	1.8.B	May not understand that the number of circles in each row should match the data provided	93	53.06
36	19.3	1.8.C	May not understand what the graph is about	99	54.06
37	20.1	1.9.A	May add the two numbers instead of counting by tens	48	3.09
38	20.2	1.9.B	May not choose the correct two items	49	3.11
39	20.3	1.9.C	May add the two numbers instead of counting by fives	43	29.29, 29.30
40	20.4	1.9.D	May count the nickels as dimes	49	3.11

*TEKS—Texas Essential Knowledge and Skills; RtI—Response to Intervention

Child's Name _____ Date _____

Middle-of-Year Test

Item	Lesson	TEKS*	Common Error	Intervene with RtI* Tier 1 Lessons	Soar to Success Math
1	1.5	1.2.B	May not include all the places in the number	5	1.15
2	1.8	1.2.C	May confuse the tens and the ones	8	2.16
3	2.4	1.2.D	May confuse greater than and less than	9	7.18
4	2.5	1.2.E	May not understand the place value of hundreds, tens, and ones	10	35.10
5	2.5	1.2.F	May confuse the meaning of least and greatest	10	35.10
6	2.2	1.2.G	May not know the difference between the symbols for greater than (>) and less than (<)	12	7.18
7	3.2	1.3.A	May count the total number of objects in the model	15	10.17
8	5.1	1.3.B	May not understand how to use a picture to subtract	20	11.04
9	4.7	1.3.C	May not understand how to add without models	26	10.14
10	7.4	1.3.D	May use the make a ten strategy incorrectly	40	11.14
11	8.1	1.3.E	May have difficulty understanding how the counters relate to the addition	44	66.01
12	8.2	1.3.F	May not understand how the addition sentence shows the situation	46	10.17

*TEKS—Texas Essential Knowledge and Skills; **RtI**—Response to Intervention

Child's Name _____ Date _____

Middle-of-Year Test (continued)

Item	Lesson	TEKS*	Common Error	Intervene with RtI* Tier 1 Lessons	Soar to Success Math
13	9.3	1.4.A	May confuse the quarter with other coins that are silver in color	50	3.10
14	9.4	1.4.C	May not understand how to show an amount in a different way	51	3.11
15	10.1	1.5.A	May start counting at 2 after 101	52	28.12
16	10.4	1.5.B	May not understand that the final number is the total number of fingers on four hands	55	31.08
17	10.7	1.5.C	May identify the number 1 less than or 1 more than another number	58	28.14
18	11.2	1.5.D	May think the missing number is the total	60	11.03
19	5.2	1.5.E	May add instead of subtracting	21	11.07
20	12.2	1.5.F	May add incorrectly	65	10.24
21	12.4	1.5.G	May not recognize the sum of the last two addends	67	10.05
22	14.1	1.6.A	May overlook "not" in the question	73	38.11
23	15.3	1.6.B	May think that color is a feature that defines a shape	76	39.13, 39.19
24	14.2	1.6.D	May think a triangle has four sides	74	38.12
25	15.2	1.6.E	May overlook "both" in the question	75	39.17, 39.26
26	14.3	1.6.F	May have difficulty visualizing a new shape composed of the same blocks	78	38.17

*TEKS—Texas Essential Knowledge and Skills; RtI—Response to Intervention

Child's Name _____ Date _____

Middle-of-Year Test (continued)

Item	Lesson	TEKS*	Common Error	Intervene with RtI* Tier 1 Lessons	Soar to Success Math
27	16.3	1.6.G	May not know that fourths and quarters are both ways to describe four equal parts	84	5.05
28	16.2	1.6.H	May overlook "not" in the question	83	5.03
29	17.1	1.7.A	May not understand the concept of comparing lengths	85	41.02
30	17.2	1.7.B	May have difficulty counting the number of tiles below the necklace	86	41.06
31	17.4	1.7.C	May think June uses the fewest of the shortest unit	88	41.06
32	17.2	1.7.D	May not count the tiles below the ribbon correctly	86	41.06
33	18.2	1.7.E	May think the clock shows time to the hour	90	51.10
34	19.7	1.8.C	May forget to subtract when comparing two numbers	97	54.04
35	19.5	1.8.A	May confuse the numbers of children who chose hopscotch and tag	95	54.03
36	19.4	1.8.B	May not be able to translate the data to a bar graph	94	53.07
37	20.1	1.9.A	May add the two numbers instead of counting by tens	48	3.09
38	20.2	1.9.B	May not choose the correct two items	49	3.11
39	20.3	1.9.C	May add instead of subtracting	43	29.29, 29.30
40	20.4	1.9.D	May count the dimes as pennies	49	3.11

*TEKS—Texas Essential Knowledge and Skills; **RtI**—Response to Intervention

End-of-Year Test

Item	Lesson	TEKS*	Common Error	Intervene with RtI* Tier 1 Lessons	Soar to Success Math
1	1.6	1.2.B	May not remove 1 tens rod after replacing it with 10 ones	6	2.19
2	1.8	1.2.C	May not understand zero as a placeholder	8	2.16
3	2.4	1.2.D	May confuse greater than and less than	9	7.18
4	2.5	1.2.E	May not understand how to use the number line to compare numbers	10	35.10
5	2.5	1.2.F	May confuse the meaning of least and greatest	10	35.10
6	2.3	1.2.G	May confuse the tens and ones for the number	13	7.15
7	3.3	1.3.A	May count the total number of objects in the model	16	10.17
8	5.4	1.3.B	May interpret the picture incorrectly	23	11.11
9	12.2	1.3.C	May add only two of the three addends	65	10.24
10	7.6	1.3.D	May not understand how to decompose a number to make a ten	42	60.02
11	8.1	1.3.E	May subtract to make a ten, and forget to subtract the rest	44	66.01
12	8.3	1.3.F	May not understand how the picture shows the subtraction fact	47	11.12

*TEKS—Texas Essential Knowledge and Skills; **RtI**—Response to Intervention

End-of-Year Test (continued)

Item	Lesson	TEKS*	Common Error	Intervene with RtI* Tier 1 Lessons	Soar to Success Math
13	9.2	1.4.A	May not understand how to show an amount in a different way	49	3.11
14	9.4	1.4.C	May incorrectly assign each dime a value of 1¢	51	3.11
15	10.2	1.5.A	May count forward instead of backward	53	28.09
16	10.5	1.5.B	May count the bags by ones	56	31.07, 33.09
17	10.7	1.5.C	May identify the number 1 less than or 1 more than another number	58	28.14
18	11.3	1.5.D	May not understand how "fewer" relates to subtraction	61	11.11
19	13.6	1.5.E	May think the missing number is the difference for 12 − 7	63	29.29, 29.30
20	13.1	1.5.F	May choose a different number from the same fact family	68	29.21, 29.32
21	13.5	1.5.G	May think the addition fact has a sum of 8 instead of 13	72	29.23
22	14.1	1.6.A	May overlook "not" in the question	73	38.11
23	15.2	1.6.B	May overlook "not" in the question	75	39.17, 39.26
24	14.2	1.6.D	May think a triangle has four sides	74	38.12
25	15.2	1.6.E	May confuse a cylinder with a cone	75	39.17, 39.26
26	14.5	1.6.F	May not be able to visualize which shapes compose a square	79	38.17

*TEKS—Texas Essential Knowledge and Skills; RtI—Response to Intervention

End-of-Year Test (continued)

Item	Lesson	TEKS*	Common Error	Intervene with RtI* Tier 1 Lessons	Soar to Success Math
27	16.3	1.6.G	May not know that fourths and quarters are both ways to describe four equal parts	84	5.05
28	16.1	1.6.H	May not be able to visualize unequal parts	82	5.03
29	17.1	1.7.A	May not understand the concept of comparing lengths	85	41.02
30	17.3	1.7.B	May have difficulty counting the number of tiles below the bracelet	87	41.06
31	17.4	1.7.C	May not understand the relationship between the size of the unit and the number of units needed to measure an object	88	41.06
32	17.3	1.7.D	May have difficulty visualizing the length of three paper clips	87	41.06
33	18.4	1.7.E	May not understand how to tell time to the half hour	92	51.08, 51.10
34	19.5	1.8.A	May not subtract when comparing two numbers	95	54.03
35	19.7	1.8.B	May not understand bar graphs	97	54.04
36	19.7	1.8.C	May have difficulty reading the questions	97	54.04
37	20.1	1.9.A	May add the two numbers instead of counting by fives	48	3.09
38	20.2	1.9.B	May not choose the correct two items	49	3.11
39	20.3	1.9.C	May solve only one step of the problem	43	29.29, 29.30
40	20.4	1.9.D	May count the 10 pennies as 1	49	3.11

*TEKS—Texas Essential Knowledge and Skills; RtI—Response to Intervention

Module 1 Test

Item	Lesson	TEKS*	Common Error	Intervene with RtI* Tier 1 Lessons	Soar to Success
1	1.1	1.2.A	May not understand that each cube represents one	1	1.13
2	1.2	1.2.A	May choose the wrong number of ones	2	1.13
3	1.3	1.2.A	May not understand that 10 ones are equal to 1 ten	3	1.16
4	1.4	1.2.B	May confuse the tens and the ones	4	1.14, 1.15
5	1.5	1.2.B	May forget to look at the number of tens	5	1.15
6	1.6	1.2.B	May not understand that 10 ones are equal to 1 ten	6	2.19
7	1.8	1.2.C	May not understand the difference between tens and ones	8	2.16
8	1.8	1.2.C	May not understand that each line in a quick picture represents 10	8	2.16
9	1.8	1.2.C	May confuse the hundreds, tens, and ones places	8	2.16
10	1.7	1.2.C	May confuse the hundreds, tens, and ones places	7	2.20
11	1.7	1.2.C	May not understand that each line in a quick picture represents 10 and each circle represents 1	7	2.20
12	1.8	1.2.C	May confuse tens and ones	8	2.16

*TEKS—Texas Essential Knowledge and Skills; **RtI**—Response to Intervention

Module 2 Test

Item	Lesson	TEKS*	Common Error	Intervene with RtI* Tier 1 Lessons	Soar to Success
1	2.4	1.2.D	May confuse greater than with less than	9	7.18
2	2.4	1.2.D	May confuse greater than with less than	9	7.18
3	2.4	1.2.E	May not understand how to use place value to compare numbers	9	7.18
4	2.4	1.2.E	May not understand the place value of tens and ones	9	7.18
5	2.5	1.2.E	May not understand the place value of hundreds, tens, and ones	10	35.10
6	2.5	1.2.F	May not understand ordering numbers	10	35.10
7	2.5	1.2.F	May confuse the meaning of least and greatest	10	35.10
8	2.5	1.2.F	May not understand how to use a number line	10	35.10
9	2.5	1.2.F	May not understand how to compare more than two numbers	10	35.10
10	2.1	1.2.G	May not remember the difference between tens and ones	11	7.18
11	2.2	1.2.G	May not understand less than	12	7.18
12	2.3	1.2.G	May not understand that equals is different from greater than or less than	13	7.15

*TEKS—Texas Essential Knowledge and Skills; RtI—Response to Intervention

Module 3 Test

Item	Lesson	TEKS*	Common Error	Intervene with RtI* Tier 1 Lessons	Soar to Success
1	3.1	1.3.A	May not understand ten frames	14	10.15
2	3.1	1.3.A	May count incorrectly	14	10.15
3	3.2	1.3.A	May confuse tens and ones	15	10.17
4	3.2	1.3.A	May not connect numbers to models	15	10.17
5	3.3	1.3.A	May confuse tens and ones	16	10.17
6	3.3	1.3.A	May confuse tens and ones	16	10.17
7	3.1	1.3.A	May not connect the model with the addition fact	14	10.15
8	3.1	1.3.A	May not understand how models show addition	14	10.15
9	3.2	1.3.A	May confuse tens and ones	15	10.17
10	3.2	1.3.A	May count the total number of objects in the model	15	10.17
11	3.3	1.3.A	May count the total number of objects in the model	16	10.17
12	3.3	1.3.A	May not distinguish tens models from ones	16	10.17

*TEKS—Texas Essential Knowledge and Skills; RtI—Response to Intervention

Module 4 Test

Item	Lesson	TEKS*	Common Error	Intervene with RtI* Tier 1 Lessons	Soar to Success
1	4.2	1.3.B	May not connect the model to the number sentence	18	10.03, 10.09
2	4.2	1.3.B	May miscount the cubes	18	10.03, 10.09
3	4.1	1.3.B	May not count both sets of objects	17	10.03
4	4.3	1.3.B	May not connect the word problem to the picture	19	10.10
5	4.6	1.3.C	May not match the addends to the model	25	10.13
6	4.7	1.3.C	May not understand how to add without models	26	10.14
7	4.5	1.3.D	May not understand the meaning of "addend"	28	10.08
8	4.3	1.5.D	May incorrectly connect model to numbers	19	10.10
9	4.3	1.5.D	May incorrectly count the objects	19	10.10
10	4.3	1.5.D	May not understand how to write a number sentence to match the problem situation	19	10.10
11	4.2	1.5.E	May not recognize that the sum will be greater than both addends	18	10.03, 10.09
12	4.4	1.5.G	May not understand how to add zero	27	10.07

*TEKS—Texas Essential Knowledge and Skills; **RtI**—Response to Intervention

Child's Name _____ Date _____

Module 5 Test

Item	Lesson	TEKS*	Common Error	Intervene with RtI* Tier 1 Lessons	Soar to Success Math
1	5.5	1.3.B	May not understand that all the birds in the picture will fly away	24	11.06
2	5.2	1.3.B	May not solve both steps of the problem	21	11.07
3	5.4	1.3.B	May not understand the meaning of "more"	23	11.11
4	5.4	1.3.B	May not understand the meaning of "fewer"	23	11.11
5	5.1	1.3.B	May not understand how to use the picture to subtract	20	11.04
6	5.2	1.3.B	May not understand how to use the picture to subtract	21	11.07
7	5.4	1.3.B	May interpret the picture incorrectly	23	11.11
8	5.4	1.3.B	May connect model to numbers incorrectly	23	11.11
9	5.6	1.3.D	May not understand that taking apart 8 subtracts from that number	29	11.03
10	5.3	1.5.D	May model the problem with two sets for the two numbers given	22	11.03
11	5.3	1.5.D	May not know how to use the picture to find the unknown	22	11.03
12	5.3	1.5.D	May add the given numbers instead of subtracting	22	11.03

*TEKS—Texas Essential Knowledge and Skills; **RtI**—Response to Intervention

Child's Name _____ Date _____

Unit 1 Test

Item	Lesson	TEKS*	Common Error	Intervene with RtI* Tier 1 Lessons	Soar to Success Math
1	1.4	1.2.B	May confuse tens and ones	4	1.14, 1.15
2	1.7	1.2.C	May not understand that the question asks for the way that does not show the number	7	2.20
3	1.8	1.2.C	May not understand that the number has hundreds, tens, and ones	8	2.16
4	1.7	1.2.C	May not understand that a number with 0 tens has no tens blocks in the model	7	2.20
5	1.8	1.2.C	May not understand zero as a placeholder	8	2.16
6	2.4	1.2.D	May confuse greater and less	9	7.18
7	2.4	1.2.D	May look at only the number of ones and not the tens	9	7.18
8	2.5	1.2.F	May incorrectly order the numbers from greatest to least	10	35.10
9	2.5	1.2.F	May not understand relative position on the number line	10	35.10
10	3.1	1.3.A	May think the model shows subtraction	14	10.15
11	5.2	1.3.B	May add to solve the word problem	21	11.07
12	5.4	1.3.B	May not know how to use the picture to compare	23	11.11
13	4.2	1.3.B	May add instead of subtracting	18	10.03, 10.09
14	4.1	1.3.B	May not understand that the picture represents addition	17	10.03

*TEKS—Texas Essential Knowledge and Skills; RtI—Response to Intervention

Child's Name _____ Date _____

Unit 1 Test (continued)

Item	Lesson	TEKS*	Common Error	Intervene with RtI* Tier 1 Lessons	Soar to Success Math
15	5.1	1.3.B	May not know how to use the picture to find the unknown	20	11.04
16	5.4	1.3.B	May identify the total number in the group with fewer items	23	11.11
17	4.3	1.5.D	May identify the model showing one group of apples	19	10.10
18	5.3	1.5.D	May add instead of subtracting	22	11.03

*TEKS—Texas Essential Knowledge and Skills; RtI—Response to Intervention

Assessment Guide
© Houghton Mifflin Harcourt Publishing Company

Individual Record Form

Module 6 Test

Item	Lesson	TEKS*	Common Error	Intervene with RtI* Tier 1 Lessons	Soar to Success Math
1	6.1	1.3.D	May start counting on with the wrong number	30	10.02
2	6.2	1.3.D	May not know the doubles facts	31	10.04
3	6.3	1.3.D	May not understand that two doubles facts may be used to solve the same problem	32	10.04
4	6.6	1.3.D	May not understand how to decompose a number to make a ten	35	10.20
5	6.1	1.3.D	May not understand that counting on is used for addition	30	10.02
6	6.2	1.3.D	May not understand the meaning of "doubles fact"	31	10.04
7	6.3	1.3.D	May forget the third addend	32	10.04
8	6.4	1.3.D	May overlook the term "not"	33	10.04
9	6.6	1.3.D	May not know how to interpret the model	35	10.20
10	6.7	1.3.D	May not know how to interpret the model	36	10.20
11	6.7	1.3.D	May not understand how to decompose a number to make a ten	36	10.20
12	6.7	1.3.D	May add incorrectly	36	10.20

*TEKS—Texas Essential Knowledge and Skills; RtI—Response to Intervention

Child's Name _____ Date _____

Module 7 Test

Item	Lesson	TEKS*	Common Error	Intervene with RtI* Tier 1 Lessons	Soar to Success Math
1	7.1	1.3.D	May start counting back from the wrong number	37	11.13
2	7.2	1.3.D	May add and not subtract the two numbers	38	29.21
3	7.3	1.3.D	May not understand that related facts use the same numbers	39	29.21
4	7.2	1.3.D	May add instead of subtracting	38	29.21
5	7.3	1.3.D	May not understand that addition undoes subtraction	39	29.21
6	7.1	1.3.D	May add instead of subtracting	37	11.13
7	7.4	1.3.D	May use the strategy of make a ten incorrectly	40	11.14
8	7.5	1.3.D	May subtract incorrectly	41	11.14
9	7.6	1.3.D	May subtract incorrectly	42	60.02
10	7.4	1.3.D	May not subtract the 1	40	11.14
11	7.5	1.3.D	May not understand how to decompose a number to make a ten	41	11.14
12	7.6	1.3.D	May identify the subtraction sentence for the second part of the model	42	60.02

*TEKS—Texas Essential Knowledge and Skills; **RtI**—Response to Intervention

Child's Name _____ Date _____

Module 8 Test

Item	Lesson	TEKS*	Common Error	Intervene with RtI* Tier 1 Lessons	Soar to Success Math
1	8.1	1.3.E	May have difficulty understanding the explanation in words	44	66.01
2	8.4	1.3.E	May not add the third addend	45	71.01
3	8.2	1.3.E	May not understand how the picture shows the addition fact	46	10.17
4	8.1	1.3.E	May mistakenly think the problem shows subtraction	44	66.01
5	8.1	1.3.E	May not understand that Jim's amount requires adding 3 + 9	44	66.01
6	8.1	1.3.E	May have difficulty understanding the explanation in words	44	66.01
7	8.4	1.3.E	May not understand that there are two steps to solve the problem	45	71.01
8	8.4	1.3.E	May add and subtract incorrectly	45	71.01
9	8.3	1.3.E	May not understand how the picture shows the subtraction fact	47	11.12
10	8.1	1.3.E	May subtract to make a ten, and forget to subtract the rest	44	66.01
11	8.2	1.3.F	May not know the words to represent addition in a word problem	46	10.17
12	8.3	1.3.F	May not know the words to represent subtraction in a word problem	47	11.12

*TEKS—Texas Essential Knowledge and Skills; **RtI**—Response to Intervention

Module 9 Test

Item	Lesson	TEKS*	Common Error	Intervene with RtI* Tier 1 Lessons	Soar to Success Math
1	9.1	1.4.A	May count one penny more than once	48	3.09
2	9.2	1.4.A	May count all coins as the same value	49	3.11
3	9.3	1.4.A	May confuse a dime with a nickel	50	3.10
4	9.3	1.4.A	May confuse the quarter with other coins that are silver in color	50	3.10
5	9.1	1.4.A	May confuse the value of a nickel with the number of coins	48	3.09
6	9.4	1.4.C	May not understand how to group the pennies by twos	51	3.11
7	9.4	1.4.C	May count the pennies in one row to find the total value	51	3.11
8	9.4	1.4.C	May add the numbers in the problem	51	3.11
9	9.4	1.4.C	May not understand how to show an amount in a different way	51	3.11
10	9.4	1.4.C	May not understand how to show an amount in a different way	51	3.11
11	9.4	1.4.C	May incorrectly assign each dime a value of 1¢	51	3.11
12	9.4	1.4.C	May not understand how to show an amount in a different way	51	3.11

*TEKS—Texas Essential Knowledge and Skills; **RtI**—Response to Intervention

Individual Record Form

Unit 2 Test

Item	Lesson	TEKS*	Common Error	Intervene with RtI*Tier 1 Lessons	Soar to Success Math
1	6.7	1.3.D	May not add the remaining number after decomposing to make a ten	36	10.20
2	7.4	1.3.D	May not understand how to interpret the model	40	11.14
3	7.5	1.3.D	May subtract 10 instead of decomposing 8	41	11.14
4	8.1	1.3.E	May not connect the words to the operations	44	66.01
5	8.1	1.3.E	May think the story shows subtraction	44	66.01
6	8.4	1.3.E	May not realize there are 2 steps needed to solve the problem	45	71.01
7	8.3	1.3.E	May subtract from the group that is not crossed out	47	11.12
8	8.1	1.3.E	May add to solve the problem instead of subtracting	44	66.01
9	8.2	1.3.F	May not know that "more" is used in an addition story	46	10.17
10	8.3	1.3.F	May not recognize the story as a subtraction situation	47	11.12
11	8.2	1.3.F	May not relate the groups in the picture to the addends in an addition sentence	46	10.17
12	8.3	1.3.F	May count the cubes in the picture incorrectly	47	11.12
13	9.3	1.4.A	May confuse the three coins since they are the same color	50	3.10
14	9.1	1.4.A	May not understand the relationship between nickels and dimes	48	3.09
15	9.2	1.4.B	May see one coin and think it has a value of 1¢	49	3.11

Unit 2 Test (continued)

Item	Lesson	TEKS*	Common Error	Intervene with RtI* Tier 1 Lessons	Soar to Success Math
16	9.4	1.4.C	May count the pennies in two groups and not groups of two	51	3.11
17	9.4	1.4.C	May not count accurately by fives	51	3.11
18	9.4	1.4.C	May not understand that 1 dime is worth the same as 10 pennies	51	3.11

*TEKS—Texas Essential Knowledge and Skills; **RtI**—Response to Intervention

Module 10 Test

Item	Lesson	TEKS*	Common Error	Intervene with RtI* Tier 1 Lessons	Soar to Success Math
1	10.1	1.5.A	May start counting at 1 after 100	52	28.12
2	10.2	1.5.A	May count forward instead of backward	53	28.09
3	10.3	1.5.B	May count the pairs by ones instead of by twos	54	31.04
4	10.3	1.5.B	May count forward by ones instead of by twos	54	31.04
5	10.4	1.5.B	May not understand that the final number is the total number of points on 13 stars	55	31.08
6	10.4	1.5.B	May count the feet by tens	55	31.08
7	10.5	1.5.B	May count the bags by ones	56	31.07, 33.09
8	10.5	1.5.B	May count the boxes incorrectly	56	31.07, 33.09
9	10.6	1.5.C	May count by ones from the last number given	57	28.14
10	10.6	1.5.C	May count forward by ones instead of by tens	57	28.14
11	10.7	1.5.C	May have difficulty counting when the numbers are near 100	58	28.14
12	10.7	1.5.C	May identify the number 1 less than or 1 more than another number	58	28.14

*TEKS—Texas Essential Knowledge and Skills; RtI—Response to Intervention

Child's Name _____ Date _____

Module 11 Test

Item	Lesson	TEKS*	Common Error	Intervene with RtI*Tier 1 Lessons	Soar to Success Math
1	11.3	1.3.B	May have difficulty understanding the model	61	11.11
2	11.3	1.3.B	May add the numbers instead of subtracting	61	11.11
3	11.1	1.5.D	May not understand how the model shows addition	59	10.03
4	11.1	1.5.D	May subtract instead of adding	59	10.03
5	11.4	1.5.D	May miscount the cubes in the model	62	29.33
6	11.1	1.5.D	May think the problem situation shows subtraction instead of addition	59	10.03
7	11.2	1.5.D	May miscount the cubes in the model	60	11.03
8	11.2	1.5.D	May think the missing number is the total	60	11.03
9	11.4	1.5.D	May not understand how the model shows subtraction	62	29.33
10	11.3	1.5.D	May not understand how "fewer" relates to subtraction	61	11.11
11	11.3	1.5.D	May subtract different numbers	61	11.11
12	11.4	1.5.D	May have difficulty understanding the model	62	29.33

*TEKS—Texas Essential Knowledge and Skills; RtI—Response to Intervention

Child's Name _____ Date _____

Module 12 Test

Item	Lesson	TEKS*	Common Error	Intervene with RtI*Tier 1 Lessons	Soar to Success Math
1	12.2	1.3.C	May add only two of the three addends	65	10.24
2	12.2	1.3.C	May not understand how the picture shows the addition fact	65	10.24
3	12.2	1.3.C	May miscount the connecting cubes	65	10.24
4	12.3	1.3.C	May add only two of the three addends	66	10.18, 10.19, 10.20, 10.24
5	12.3	1.3.C	May add only two of the three addends	66	10.18, 10.19, 10.20, 10.24
6	12.3	1.3.C	May add incorrectly	66	10.18, 10.19, 10.20, 10.24
7	12.4	1.5.F	May add incorrectly	67	10.05
8	12.1	1.5.G	May match only the sum and not the addends	64	10.08
9	12.1	1.5.G	May confuse the order of the addends and choose the identical fact	64	10.08
10	12.4	1.5.G	May only add two of the addends	67	10.05
11	12.4	1.5.G	May add only two of the three addends	67	10.05
12	12.4	1.5.G	May not understand that all three numbers are added to answer the question	67	10.05

*TEKS—Texas Essential Knowledge and Skills; RtI—Response to Intervention

Child's Name _____   Date _____

Module 13 Test

Item	Lesson	TEKS*	Common Error	Intervene with RtI* Tier 1 Lessons	Soar to Success Math
1	13.6	1.5.E	May think the missing number is the difference for 17 – 8	63	29.29, 29.30
2	13.1	1.5.F	May choose a different number from the same fact family	68	29.21, 29.32
3	13.2	1.5.F	May subtract 7 and 5 instead of adding them	69	29.31
4	13.4	1.5.F	May not understand that the same number is the unknown in both related sentences	71	29.21
5	13.3	1.5.F	May not have memorized doubles facts	70	29.21
6	13.5	1.5.F	May mistakenly think about making a ten to subtract	72	29.23
7	13.1	1.5.G	May subtract 7 and 8 instead of adding them	68	29.21, 29.32
8	13.2	1.5.G	May subtract a different number from 13	69	29.31
9	13.3	1.5.G	May not understand how addition can check subtraction	70	29.21
10	13.4	1.5.G	May choose the wrong number in the fact family	71	29.21
11	13.4	1.5.G	May not understand that there are two steps to solve the story problem	71	29.21
12	13.5	1.5.G	May think the addition fact has a sum of 6 instead of 15	72	29.23

*TEKS—Texas Essential Knowledge and Skills; RtI—Response to Intervention

Child's Name _____ Date _____

Unit 3 Test

Item	Lesson	TEKS*	Common Error	Intervene with RtI* Tier 1 Lessons	Soar to Success Math
1	11.3	1.3.B	May have difficulty understanding the model	61	11.11
2	12.2	1.3.C	May only add two of the three addends	65	10.24
3	12.2	1.3.C	May not understand how the picture shows the addition fact	65	10.24
4	12.3	1.3.C	May add incorrectly	66	10.18, 10.19, 10.20, 10.24
5	10.4	1.5.B	May not understand that the final number is the total number of fingers on 12 hands	55	31.08
6	10.5	1.5.B	May mistakenly count the bags by ones	56	31.07, 33.09
7	10.7	1.5.C	May mistakenly identify the number right before or after	58	28.14
8	11.1	1.5.D	May subtract instead of adding to solve the problem	59	10.03
9	11.4	1.5.D	May miscount the cubes in the model	62	29.33
10	11.1	1.5.D	May think the problem situation shows subtraction instead of addition	59	10.03
11	11.2	1.5.D	May think the missing number is the total	60	11.03
12	11.4	1.5.D	May not understand how the model shows subtraction	62	29.33
13	11.2	1.5.D	May subtract the two given numbers	60	11.03

*TEKS—Texas Essential Knowledge and Skills; **RtI**—Response to Intervention

Unit 3 Test (continued)

Item	Lesson	TEKS*	Common Error	Intervene with RtI* Tier 1 Lessons	Soar to Success Math
14	11.3	1.5.D	May get an answer of 2 by subtracting different numbers	61	11.11
15	13.6	1.5.E	May make 9 an addend instead of the sum	63	29.29, 29.30
16	13.1	1.5.F	May not understand that the same number is the unknown in all related sentences	68	29.21, 29.32
17	12.4	1.5.G	May add incorrectly	67	10.05
18	13.5	1.5.G	May mistakenly make a ten to add	72	29.23

*TEKS—Texas Essential Knowledge and Skills; RtI—Response to Intervention

Assessment Guide
© Houghton Mifflin Harcourt Publishing Company

Individual Record Form

Module 14 Test

Item	Lesson	TEKS*	Common Error	Intervene with RtI* Tier 1 Lessons	Soar to Success Math
1	14.5	1.6.C	May see curves on quarter circles and think they make a whole circle	79	38.17
2	14.5	1.6.C	May think a trapezoid is part of the triangle since they look alike	79	38.17
3	14.5	1.6.C	May have difficulty visualizing how to combine shapes	79	38.17
4	14.5	1.6.C	May overlook "not" in the question	79	38.17
5	14.3	1.6.C	May have difficulty visualizing how to put the triangles together	78	38.17
6	14.1	1.6.D	May think the rhombus is a triangle since it is composed of 2 triangles	73	38.11
7	14.2	1.6.D	May be confused since rectangle is not an answer choice	74	38.12
8	14.1	1.6.D	May think the heart is a circle since it is closed and has curves	73	38.11
9	14.2	1.6.D	May mistakenly think a triangle has 4 sides	74	38.12
10	14.2	1.6.D	May confuse a hexagon with a pentagon	74	38.12
11	14.4	1.6.F	May mistakenly think that the triangle is a right triangle	81	38.17
12	14.3	1.6.F	May not understand that the new shape should be composed of 3 rhombuses	78	38.17

*TEKS—Texas Essential Knowledge and Skills; RtI—Response to Intervention

Child's Name _____ Date _____

Module 15 Test

Item	Lesson	TEKS*	Common Error	Intervene with RtI* Tier 1 Lessons	Soar to Success Math
1	15.3	1.6.B	May mistakenly think that size and color are features that define a shape	76	39.13, 39.19
2	15.2	1.6.E	May overlook "not" in the question	75	39.17, 39.26
3	15.1	1.6.E	May overlook "not" in the question	80	39.34
4	15.2	1.6.E	May not know which shape is a sphere since they all have a curved surface	75	39.17, 39.26
5	15.4	1.6.E	May confuse a cone, a cylinder, and a cube	77	39.13
6	15.4	1.6.E	May not understand that a triangular prism has flat surfaces that are triangles	77	39.13
7	15.2	1.6.E	May not understand that a solid can have no flat surfaces	75	39.17, 39.26
8	15.2	1.6.E	May overlook "both" in the question	75	39.17, 39.26
9	15.2	1.6.E	May think all blocks are rectangular prisms	75	39.17, 39.26
10	15.3	1.6.E	May think that a triangular prism is the same as a rectangular prism	76	39.13, 39.19
11	15.3	1.6.E	May be confused since the rectangular prism has some faces that are squares and some that are rectangles	76	39.13, 39.19
12	15.3	1.6.E	May not know the meaning of "edge"	76	39.13, 39.19

*TEKS—Texas Essential Knowledge and Skills; **RtI**—Response to Intervention

Child's Name _____ Date _____

Module 16 Test

Item	Lesson	TEKS*	Common Error	Intervene with RtI* Tier 1 Lessons	Soar to Success Math
1	16.1	1.6.G	May not be able to visualize which shape shows equal parts and which does not	82	5.03
2	16.1	1.6.G	May not be able to visualize which shape shows equal parts and which does not	82	5.03
3	16.2	1.6.G	May think that any straight line divides a circle into equal parts	83	5.03
4	16.3	1.6.G	May mistakenly choose the circle with two equal shares	84	5.05
5	16.3	1.6.G	May not know that a fourth and a quarter are both ways to describe one of four equal parts	84	5.05
6	16.3	1.6.G	May not know that a fourth is one of four equal parts	84	5.05
7	16.2	1.6.H	May think halves show three equal parts	83	5.03
8	16.3	1.6.H	May mistakenly think that every shape with four parts shows fourths	84	5.05
9	16.2	1.6.H	May overlook "not" in the question	83	5.03
10	16.2	1.6.H	May overlook "not" in the question	83	5.03
11	16.3	1.6.H	May overlook "not" in the question	84	5.05
12	16.3	1.6.H	May not know that a shape with fourths needs to have four equal parts	84	5.05

*TEKS—Texas Essential Knowledge and Skills; RtI—Response to Intervention

Module 17 Test

Item	Lesson	TEKS*	Common Error	Intervene with RtI* Tier 1 Lessons	Soar to Success Math
1	17.1	1.7.A	May not understand the concept of comparing lengths	85	41.02
2	17.2	1.7.B	May have difficulty counting the number of tiles below the marker	86	41.06
3	17.3	1.7.B	May miscount the paper clips	87	41.06
4	17.4	1.7.C	May think that the longest unit would require the most units to measure the object	88	41.06
5	17.4	1.7.C	May think that the shortest unit would require the fewest units to measure the object	88	41.06
6	17.4	1.7.C	May not understand the relationship between the size of the unit and the number of units needed to measure an object	88	41.06
7	17.4	1.7.C	May think that the longest unit would require the most units to measure the object	88	41.06
8	17.4	1.7.C	May think that the longest unit would require the most units to measure the object	88	41.06
9	17.4	1.7.C	May think Matt uses the fewest of the shortest unit	88	41.06
10	17.2	1.7.D	May think that 2 tiles in length is a long measurement	86	41.06
11	17.2	1.7.D	May think that 4 tiles is the shortest length	86	41.06
12	17.3	1.7.D	May have difficulty visualizing the lengths of the real objects	87	41.06

*TEKS—Texas Essential Knowledge and Skills; RtI—Response to Intervention

Child's Name _____ Date _____

Module 18 Test

Item	Lesson	TEKS*	Common Error	Intervene with RtI* Tier 1 Lessons	Soar to Success Math
1	18.1	1.7.E	May confuse the hour hand and minute hand	89	51.08
2	18.1	1.7.E	May not understand where the hour hand is pointing	89	51.08
3	18.1	1.7.E	May not be able to determine where the hour hands point on the clocks	89	51.08
4	18.3	1.7.E	May not understand that the hour hand points to the hour and the minute hand points to 12	91	51.08, 51.10
5	18.3	1.7.E	May not understand how to relate analog and digital time	91	51.08, 51.10
6	18.3	1.7.E	May not understand that "o'clock" can replace "00"	91	51.08, 51.10
7	18.2	1.7.E	May not understand how to tell time to the half hour	90	51.10
8	18.2	1.7.E	May not know that "half past 11" is the same as 11:30	90	51.10
9	18.2	1.7.E	May think the clock shows time to the hour	90	51.10
10	18.4	1.7.E	May not understand how to tell time to the half hour	92	51.08, 51.10
11	18.4	1.7.E	May think the hour hand is pointing to 8	92	51.08, 51.10
12	18.4	1.7.E	May not understand how to tell time to the half hour	92	51.08, 51.10

*TEKS—Texas Essential Knowledge and Skills; RtI—Response to Intervention

Unit 4 Test

Item	Lesson	TEKS*	Common Error	Intervene with RtI* Tier 1 Lessons	Soar to Success Math
1	14.3	1.6.C	May have difficulty visualizing how to put the triangles together	78	38.17
2	14.2	1.6.D	May not know that a square has four sides of equal length	74	38.12
3	14.2	1.6.D	May think a triangle has four or five sides	74	38.12
4	14.2	1.6.D	May miscount the sides and vertices	74	38.12
5	15.2	1.6.E	May not understand that a solid can have no flat surfaces	75	39.17, 39.26
6	15.2	1.6.E	May not recognize that the question asks for a solid with only one flat surface	75	39.17, 39.26
7	15.2	1.6.E	May confuse a cylinder and a cone	75	39.17, 39.26
8	14.3	1.6.F	May not understand that the shape is composed of 2 triangles and a rhombus	78	38.17
9	16.2	1.6.G	May not be able to visualize which shape shows equal parts and which does not	83	5.03
10	16.2	1.6.G	May not be able to visualize which shape shows equal parts and which does not	83	5.03
11	16.3	1.6.G	May not know that fourths and quarters are both ways to describe four equal parts	84	5.05
12	16.3	1.6.G	May not be able to visualize which shape shows equal parts and which does not	84	5.05

*TEKS—Texas Essential Knowledge and Skills; RtI—Response to Intervention

Unit 4 Test (continued)

Item	Lesson	TEKS*	Common Error	Intervene with RtI* Tier 1 Lessons	Soar to Success Math
13	16.3	1.6.H	May not recognize that the triangle shows unequal parts	84	5.05
14	17.4	1.7.C	May think that the shortest unit would require the fewest units to measure the object	88	41.06
15	18.1	1.7.E	May not understand how the hour hand indicates time	89	51.08
16	18.3	1.7.E	May not understand that "o'clock" stands for "00"	91	51.08, 51.10
17	18.2	1.7.E	May not understand how to tell time to the half hour	90	51.10
18	18.4	1.7.E	May not understand how to tell time to the half hour	92	51.08, 51.10

*TEKS—Texas Essential Knowledge and Skills; **RtI**—Response to Intervention

Unit 5 Test

Item	Lesson	TEKS*	Common Error	Intervene with RtI* Tier 1 Lessons	Soar to Success Math
1	19.6	1.8.A	May not realize that the correct table shows the numbers of boys and girls in the class	96	54.10
2	19.6	1.8.A	May not realize that the correct table shows different colors of crayons	96	54.10
3	19.6	1.8.A	May miscount the pieces of fruit	96	54.10
4	19.5	1.8.A	May not understand that the number of tally marks should be greater for pizza than for pasta	95	54.03
5	19.5	1.8.A	May confuse the numbers of children who chose popcorn and chips	95	54.03
6	19.5	1.8.A	May forget that the total number of tally marks should be 10	95	54.03
7	19.5	1.8.A	May miscount the tally marks	95	54.03
8	19.5	1.8.A	May not find the difference of the two numbers	95	54.03
9	19.2	1.8.B	May not understand that the number of circles in each row should match the data provided	93	53.06
10	19.4	1.8.B	May not understand how to read bar graphs	94	53.07
11	19.1	1.8.C	May not understand how to read picture graphs	98	54.05

*TEKS—Texas Essential Knowledge and Skills; RtI—Response to Intervention

Unit 5 Test (continued)

Item	Lesson	TEKS*	Common Error	Intervene with RtI* Tier 1 Lessons	Soar to Success Math
12	19.2	1.8.C	May not understand what the graph is about	93	53.06
13	19.1	1.8.C	May count the symbols in the wrong row	98	54.05
14	19.3	1.8.C	May confuse the most with the fewest	99	54.06
15	19.3	1.8.C	May confuse the most with the fewest	99	54.06
16	19.7	1.8.C	May not understand what the graph is about	97	54.04
17	19.7	1.8.C	May not know how to read a vertical bar graph	97	54.04
18	19.7	1.8.C	May add incorrectly	97	54.04

*TEKS—Texas Essential Knowledge and Skills; RtI—Response to Intervention

Unit 6 Test

Item	Lesson	TEKS*	Common Error	Intervene with RtI* Tier 1 Lessons	Soar to Success Math
1	20.1	1.9.A	May add the two numbers instead of counting by tens	48	3.09
2	20.1	1.9.A	May add the two numbers instead of counting by fives	48	3.09
3	20.1	1.9.A	May add or subtract the two numbers	48	3.09
4	20.2	1.9.B	May not understand the difference between wants and needs	49	3.11
5	20.2	1.9.B	May not understand the difference between wants and needs	49	3.11
6	20.2	1.9.B	May not choose the correct two items	49	3.11
7	20.2	1.9.B	May not choose the correct two items	49	3.11
8	20.2	1.9.B	May not understand the difference between goods and services	49	3.11
9	20.2	1.9.B	May not understand the difference between goods and services	49	3.11
10	20.3	1.9.C	May not understand the concept of spending money	43	29.29, 29.30
11	20.3	1.9.C	May count by fives incorrectly	43	29.29, 29.30

*TEKS—Texas Essential Knowledge and Skills; RtI—Response to Intervention

Unit 6 Test (continued)

Item	Lesson	TEKS*	Common Error	Intervene with RtI* Tier 1 Lessons	Soar to Success Math
12	20.3	1.9.C	May add instead of subtracting	43	29.29, 29.30
13	20.3	1.9.C	May not understand the concept of saving money	43	29.29, 29.30
14	20.3	1.9.C	May add the two numbers instead of counting by fives	43	29.29, 29.30
15	20.3	1.9.C	May solve only one step of the problem	43	29.29, 29.30
16	20.4	1.9.D	May count the nickel as a dime or a penny	49	3.11
17	20.4	1.9.D	May count the nickels as dimes	49	3.11
18	20.4	1.9.D	May count the nickels as pennies	49	3.11

*TEKS—Texas Essential Knowledge and Skills; RtI—Response to Intervention

Correlations

	Texas Essential Knowledge and Skills for Mathematics	Test: Item Numbers
1.2	**Number and operations.** The student applies mathematical process standards to represent and compare whole numbers, the relative position and magnitude of whole numbers, and relationships within the numeration system related to place value. The student is expected to:	
1.2.A	recognize instantly the quantity of structured arrangements;	Module 1 Test: 1–3
1.2.B	use concrete and pictorial models to compose and decompose numbers up to 120 in more than one way as so many hundreds, so many tens, and so many ones;	Module 1 Test: 4–6 Unit 1 Test: 1 Beginning-/Middle-/End-of-Year Tests: 1
1.2.C	use objects, pictures, and expanded and standard forms to represent numbers up to 120;	Module 1 Test: 7–12 Unit 1 Test: 2–5 Beginning-/Middle-/End-of-Year Tests: 2
1.2.D	generate a number that is greater than or less than a given whole number up to 120;	Module 2 Test: 1–2 Unit 1 Test: 6–7 Beginning-/Middle-/End-of-Year Tests: 3
1.2.E	use place value to compare whole numbers up to 120 using comparative language;	Module 2 Test: 3–5 Beginning-/Middle-/End-of-Year Tests: 4
1.2.F	order whole numbers up to 120 using place value and open number lines; and	Module 2 Test: 6–9 Unit 1 Test: 8–9 Beginning-/Middle-/End-of-Year Tests: 5
1.2.G	represent the comparison of two numbers to 100 using the symbols $>$, $<$, or $=$.	Module 2 Test: 10–12 Beginning-/Middle-/End-of-Year Tests: 6
1.3	**Number and operations.** The student applies mathematical process standards to develop and use strategies for whole number addition and subtraction computations in order to solve problems. The student is expected to:	
1.3.A	use concrete and pictorial models to determine the sum of a multiple of 10 and a one-digit number in problems up to 99;	Module 3 Test: 1–12 Unit 1 Test: 10 Beginning-/Middle-/End-of-Year Tests: 7
1.3.B	use objects and pictorial models to solve word problems involving joining, separating, and comparing sets within 20 and unknowns as any one of the terms in the problem such as $2 + 4 = [\ ]$; $3 + [\ ] = 7$; and $5 = [\ ] - 3$;	Module 4 Test: 1–4 Module 5 Test: 1–8 Unit 1 Test: 11–16 Module 11 Test: 1–2 Unit 3 Test: 1 Beginning-/Middle-/End-of-Year Tests: 8
1.3.C	compose 10 with two or more addends with and without concrete objects;	Module 4 Test: 5–6 Module 12 Test: 1–6 Unit 3 Test: 2–4 Beginning-/Middle-/End-of-Year Tests: 9

Correlations

Texas Essential Knowledge and Skills for Mathematics		Test: Item Numbers
1.3.D	apply basic fact strategies to add and subtract within 20, including making 10 and decomposing a number leading to a 10;	Module 4 Test: 7–10 Module 5 Test: 9 Module 6 Test: 1–12 Module 7 Test: 1–12 Unit 2 Test: 1–3 Beginning-/Middle-/End-of-Year Tests: 10
1.3.E	explain strategies used to solve addition and subtraction problems up to 20 using spoken words, objects, pictorial models, and number sentences; and	Module 8 Test: 1–10 Unit 2 Test: 4–8 Beginning-/Middle-/End-of-Year Tests: 11
1.3.F	generate and solve problem situations when given a number sentence involving addition or subtraction of numbers within 20.	Module 8 Test: 11–12 Unit 2 Test: 9–12 Beginning-/Middle-/End-of-Year Tests: 12
1.4	**Number and operations.** The student applies mathematical process standards to identify coins, their values, and the relationships among them in order to recognize the need for monetary transactions. The student is expected to:	
1.4.A	identify U.S. coins, including pennies, nickels, dimes, and quarters, by value and describe the relationships among them;	Module 9 Test: 1–5 Unit 2 Test: 13–14 Beginning-/Middle-/End-of-Year Tests: 13
1.4.B	write a number with the cent symbol to describe the value of a coin; and	Unit 2 Test: 15
1.4.C	use relationships to count by twos, fives, and tens to determine the value of a collection of pennies, nickels, and/or dimes.	Module 9 Test: 6–12 Unit 2 Test: 16–18 Beginning-/Middle-/End-of-Year Tests: 14
1.5	**Algebraic reasoning.** The student applies mathematical process standards to identify and apply number patterns within properties of numbers and operations in order to describe relationships. The student is expected to:	
1.5.A	recite numbers forward and backward from any given number between 1 and 120;	Module 10 Test: 1–2 Beginning-/Middle-/End-of-Year Tests: 15
1.5.B	skip count by twos, fives, and tens to determine the total number of objects up to 120 in a set;	Module 10 Test: 3–8 Unit 3 Test: 5–6 Beginning-/Middle-/End-of-Year Tests: 16
1.5.C	use relationships to determine the number that is 10 more and 10 less than a given number up to 120;	Module 10 Test: 9–12 Unit 3 Test: 7 Beginning-/Middle-/End-of-Year Tests: 17
1.5.D	represent word problems involving addition and subtraction of whole numbers up to 20 using concrete and pictorial models and number sentences;	Module 4 Test: 8–10 Module 5 Test: 10–12 Unit 1 Test: 17–18 Module 11 Test: 3–12 Unit 3 Test: 8–14 Beginning-/Middle-/End-of-Year Tests: 18

Correlations

Texas Essential Knowledge and Skills for Mathematics		Test: Item Numbers
1.5.E	understand that the equal sign represents a relationship where expressions on each side of the equal sign represent the same value(s);	Module 4 Test: 11 Module 13 Test: 1 Unit 3 Test: 15 Beginning-/Middle-/End-of-Year Tests: 19
1.5.F	determine the unknown whole number in an addition or subtraction equation when the unknown may be any one of the three or four terms in the equation; and	Module 12 Test: 7 Module 13 Test: 2–6 Unit 3 Test: 16 Beginning-/Middle-/End-of-Year Tests: 20
1.5.G	apply properties of operations to add and subtract two or three numbers.	Module 4 Test: 12 Module 12 Test: 8–12 Module 13 Test: 7–12 Unit 3 Test: 17–18 Beginning-/Middle-/End-of-Year Tests: 21
1.6	**Geometry and measurement.** The student applies mathematical process standards to analyze attributes of two-dimensional shapes and three-dimensional solids to develop generalizations about their properties. The student is expected to:	
1.6.A	classify and sort regular and irregular two-dimensional shapes based on attributes using informal geometric language;	Beginning-/Middle-/End-of-Year Tests: 22
1.6.B	distinguish between attributes that define a two-dimensional or three-dimensional figure and attributes that do not define the shape;	Module 15 Test: 1–2 Beginning-/Middle-/End-of-Year Tests: 23
1.6.C	create two-dimensional figures, including circles, triangles, rectangles, and squares, as special rectangles, rhombuses, and hexagons;	Module 14 Test: 1–5 Unit 4 Test: 1
1.6.D	identify two-dimensional shapes, including circles, triangles, rectangles, and squares, as special rectangles, rhombuses, and hexagons and describe their attributes using formal geometric language;	Module 14 Test: 6–10 Unit 4 Test: 2–4 Beginning-/Middle-/End-of-Year Tests: 24
1.6.E	identify three-dimensional solids, including spheres, cones, cylinders, rectangular prisms (including cubes), and triangular prisms, and describe their attributes using formal geometric language;	Module 15 Test: 3–12 Unit 4 Test: 5–7 Beginning-/Middle-/End-of-Year Tests: 25
1.6.F	compose two-dimensional shapes by joining two, three, or four figures to produce a target shape in more than one way if possible;	Module 14 Test: 11–12 Unit 4 Test: 8 Beginning-/Middle-/End-of-Year Tests: 26
1.6.G	partition two-dimensional figures into two and four fair shares or equal parts and describe the parts using words; and	Module 16 Test: 1–6 Unit 4 Test: 9–12 Beginning-/Middle-/End-of-Year Tests: 27
1.6.H	identify examples and non-examples of halves and fourths.	Module 16 Test: 7–12 Unit 4 Test: 13 Beginning-/Middle-/End-of-Year Tests: 28

Correlations

Texas Essential Knowledge and Skills for Mathematics		Test: Item Numbers
1.7	**Geometry and measurement.** The student applies mathematical process standards to select and use units to describe length and time. The student is expected to:	
1.7.A	use measuring tools to measure the length of objects to reinforce the continuous nature of linear measurement;	Module 17 Test: 1 Beginning-/Middle-/End-of-Year Tests: 29
1.7.B	illustrate that the length of an object is the number of same-size units of length that, when laid end-to-end with no gaps or overlaps, reach from one end of the object to the other;	Module 17 Test: 2–3 Beginning-/Middle-/End-of-Year Tests: 30
1.7.C	measure the same object/distance with units of two different lengths and describe how and why the measurements differ;	Module 17 Test: 4–9 Unit 4 Test: 14 Beginning-/Middle-/End-of-Year Tests: 31
1.7.D	describe a length to the nearest whole unit using a number and a unit; and	Module 17 Test: 10–12 Beginning-/Middle-/End-of-Year Tests: 32
1.7.E	tell time to the hour and half hour using analog and digital clocks.	Module 18 Test: 1–12 Unit 4 Test: 15–18 Beginning-/Middle-/End-of-Year Tests: 33
1.8	**Data analysis.** The student applies mathematical process standards to organize data to make it useful for interpreting information and solving problems. The student is expected to:	
1.8.A	collect, sort, and organize data in up to three categories using models/representations such as tally marks or T-charts;	Unit 5 Test: 1–8 Beginning-/Middle-/End-of-Year Tests: 34
1.8.B	use data to create picture and bar-type graphs; and	Unit 5 Test: 9–10 Beginning-/Middle-/End-of-Year Tests: 35
1.8.C	draw conclusions and generate and answer questions using information from picture and bar-type graphs.	Unit 5 Test: 11–18 Beginning-/Middle-/End-of-Year Tests: 36
1.9	**Personal financial literacy.** The student applies mathematical process standards to manage one's financial resources effectively for lifetime financial security. The student is expected to:	
1.9.A	define money earned as income;	Unit 6 Test: 1–3 Beginning-/Middle-/End-of-Year Tests: 37
1.9.B	identify income as a means of obtaining goods and services, oftentimes making choices between wants and needs;	Unit 6 Test: 4–9 Beginning-/Middle-/End-of-Year Tests: 38
1.9.C	distinguish between spending and saving; and	Unit 6 Test: 10–15 Beginning-/Middle-/End-of-Year Tests: 39
1.9.D	consider charitable giving.	Unit 6 Test: 16–18 Beginning-/Middle-/End-of-Year Tests: 40

Assessment Guide
© Houghton Mifflin Harcourt Publishing Company

AG189

Correlations